NARROW BOATS

Care and Maintenance

Narrow Boats
Care and Maintenance

NICK BILLINGHAM

The Crowood Press

First published in 1995 by
The Crowood Press Ltd
Ramsbury, Marlborough
Wiltshire SN8 2HR

www.crowood.com

This impression 2016

British Library Cataloguing-in-Publication Data
A catalogue record for this book is available from the British
Library.

ISBN 978 1 85223 861 2

Dedication
This book is dedicated to my wife Sonia, who has had to cope with
taking second place to my boat since she was eighteen!

This book is intended to be used for guidance only. All work
carried out on a boat must be in accordance with the relevant
manufacturer's or builder's specification and comply with the
relevant codes of practice and safety procedures.

Please note that the provisions of the Boat Safety Scheme described
in Chapter 7 have changed since this book was first published, and
remain in a state of some flux. The reader is advised to ensure that
he follows the standards currently in force at any particular time.
Current details of the Boat Safety Scheme can be downloaded from
www.boatsafetyscheme.com.

Picture Credits
All photographs by Nick Billingham
Line-drawings by Bob Constant

Typeset by Phoenix Typesetting, Ilkley, West Yorkshire
Printed and bound in India by Replika Press Pvt. Ltd.

Contents

Acknowledgements

I would like to thank the following companies and people for their help towards producing this book: British Waterways, particularly for their help in explaining the Boat Safety Scheme; Black Country Narrowboats; Midland Canal Centre; Warwickshire Fly Boat Company; Wombourne Canal & Leisure Services; and to the many patient boat owners who have allowed their boats to be photographed – thanks for the tea!

Preface

This is a book for people with narrow boats. Unlike river cruisers or offshore boats, narrow boats have their own special needs, and were evolved to cruise on waterways that were built before the age of steam, long before trains and cars. Now, the canals provide a very special way for all of us to appreciate not only the beauty of the country that we live in, but the work and energy that our ancestors invested in their businesses. They created a transport system that gave the Industrial Revolution the chance it needed to make England one of the richest countries in the world. For nearly a hundred years the canals were the principal means of heavy goods transport.

As the role of the narrow boat declined, a new culture was born. Boatmen were forced to move their families out of ordinary houses on to their boats, and in this small and enclosed world a new type of art flourished. Boats were gaily painted, but this in fact masked the very real poverty of families struggling to find cargoes in the face of competition from the railways. The railways bought up the canals, too, and often allowed them to decline. Maintenance standards dropped, and weeds grew across the once bright waters.

Luckily the canals were rescued from dereliction by a handful of people who realized their value, both as fascinating artefacts of our industrial heritage, and as a living world of wildlife, boats and leisure activity. The Inland Waterways Association fought for the restoration of all our canals, and still does, and it is thanks to their tireless efforts that the tide of public opinion has turned. Where councils and planners once viewed our canals as dangerous and polluted nuisances, they now see opportunities for waterside developments and recreational space. Our boats are part of this heritage: without the boats the canals are pointless and would be choked by weeds; with them, they bring life into the darkest corners of industrial wastelands.

Most boaters are fairly practical; boating is very much a hands-on activity, especially if there's a mattress wrapped round the propeller! This book will, I hope, provide a structure to the maintenance schedule of the narrow-boat enthusiast so that boats can cruise more reliably and safely and provide even more pleasure.

Safety is an important aspect of any vehicle, and yet the introduction of safety standards for narrow boats has been fraught with difficulty. A large part of Chapter 7 is devoted to the current Boat Safety Scheme in an attempt to explain and clarify it. Boating accidents are in fact very rare, but it is in all our interests to reduce their likelihood even more.

Introduction

The narrow boat represents a delightful way to explore the rivers and canals of Britain. From the industrial heartlands of our cities to the tranquillity of the countryside, they can cruise along more than 2,000 miles of waterways. The boats themselves have come a long way from their industrial ancestors; instead of heavy goods they now carry people in a luxury that the old boatmen would find hard to imagine.

A modern, well equipped boat frequently has a microwave cooker, a washing machine, and all the comforts of a country cottage. The engines have evolved, too: horses and steam gave way to the hot-bulb oil engine and finally to the modern, high-speed diesel engine that provides power quietly and efficiently at the turn of a key. Gas cookers, radios, televisions, more and more sophisticated systems are available to make boating more comfortable – unless they break down!

Narrow boats come in a variety of shapes and sizes. The four main types are: Trad, short for traditional; Cruiser, an ordinary hull with a modern cabin and plenty of deck space; Semi-Trad, a cross between the two; and Tug, which is a more complicated version of the Trad boat based on an idealized notion of the old Birmingham tugs. 'Idealized' is certainly the word, too, because most Birmingham Tugs were working boats that had become too battered to carry any more cargo, had been shortened by thirty feet (9m), and had had a lorry engine shoe-horned into the engine hole.

There are endless arguments about just what a proper, traditional boat should look like. The original carrying companies like Fellows, Morton & Clayton, and others, built their own boats to their own designs, and they could be dramatically different. For the purists, the argument is easily settled: if the boat can't take twenty tons of cargo, it just isn't traditional.

Each variety of boat has its advantages. If you have a large circle of friends and relations, the ample deck space afforded by the Cruiser makes for very sociable cruising. If you need to fence in younger children, then the Semi-Trad offers a big deck with an effective toddler-proof fence. The Traditional offers by far the most cabin space and is popular with people who like to spend months exploring the waterways, taking most of their possessions with them. Regardless of the shape, the systems that make each boat go are the same for all the different styles; the steelwork suffers from the same sort of rust, and they all go through the same locks.

A boat is a fairly complicated device, and it needs to be looked after to work at its best. No one would dream of running a car for ten years without checking that everything still worked correctly, and the same holds true for narrow boats. Well cared for, a modern boat will last fifty years, and it could well hold its value for most of that period, too; neglected, a boat soon starts to depreciate, and holidays become a battle to make repairs when equipment breaks rather than being able to enjoy the relaxing pace of the cut.

The reasons for a maintenance schedule for a boat are clear: the various systems and structure are likely to fail if they are not

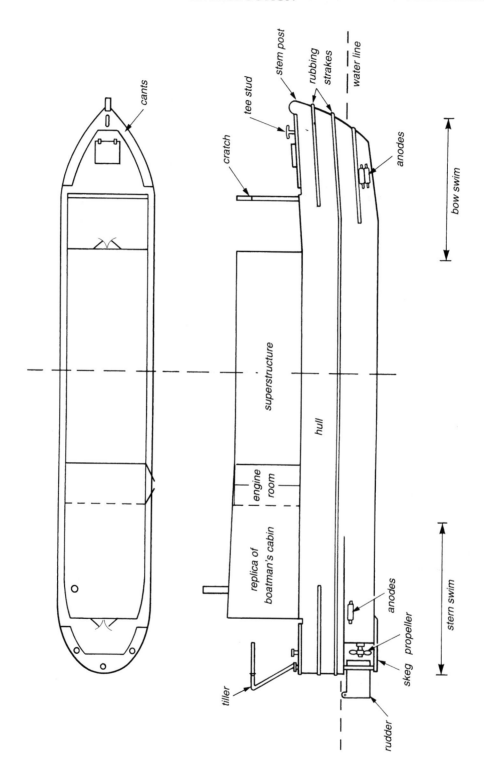

Modern narrow boat built on traditional lines.

cants

stem post

rubbing
strakes

water line

tee stud

cratch

anodes

bow swim

superstructure

hull

engine
room

replica of
boatman's cabin

anodes

stern swim

skeg   propeller

tiller

rudder

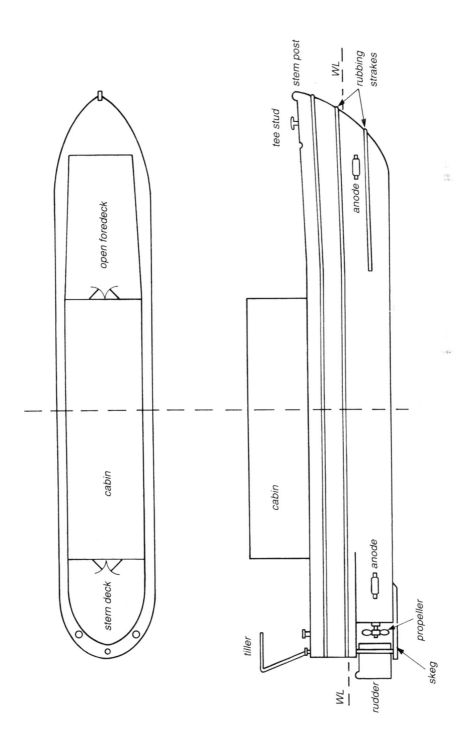

Modern narrow boat, Cruiser style.

looked after. Even a little thing like a fuel filter can spoil your cruising; a bit of dirt gets through, clogs up the engine and there you are, drifting along with no power. Probably it will then start to rain, there won't be anyone in miles to clean the dirt out of the injectors, and a thoroughly miserable time will be had by all. More importantly, if the engine fails as you are navigating a large river it could endanger the lives of everyone on board.

The care of a narrow boat is not particularly difficult, and is largely a matter of common sense and practicality. For the most part the boats are built with safety, simplicity and strength in mind – if they built cars the way they build narrow boats, we would all be driving around in tanks! At first sight the number of different systems in a boat can seem daunting, but each system can be clearly identified and inspected, and a regular programme of cleaning and servicing will ensure the boat is always ready to take you on a cruise. There are a couple of time-honoured engineers' sayings always worth bearing in mind:

'If a job's worth doing, it's worth doing properly', and this is very apt for boats. It can take the best part of a morning to service the engine, but if the job is done well it should be all that is needed for months. It will take just as long to do it badly or with second-rate oil and filters, but in this case it will probably need to be done all over again within a month. The same is true of construction: it costs a little more to use stainless steel screws and bolts, but these will last ten times longer than cheap ones.

'If it ain't broke, don't fix it.' This is a common enough saying in the Black Country, meaning that machines are put together to work, not to be stripped down and tinkered with needlessly. Nowadays many pumps and fittings are made from plastic parts held together with self-tapping screws; the more often they are dismantled, the greater the wear on the threads, and once the threads

are worn out the whole thing is only fit for the dustbin. The same is true for metal engines, although the process takes a lot longer.

This book is all about caring for a narrow boat, and the systems that supply water, light and heat are fairly standard. The main drawback is that no two boats have ever been built the same. Narrow boats vary in size from the tiny, 18ft long model, to a lock-filling 72ft; the only common denominator is the word 'narrow', and any boat more than about 7ft 2in wide won't be going that far. There are converted workboats that started life carrying coal, oil or even gravel, whose most luxurious fitting is a battery-powered radio, and there are boats for living in with all mod cons including central heating and a jacuzzi. As a result, the fittings and appliances can be just about anywhere; simply finding where the wires and gas pipes go in an older boat can be a day's work, never mind about finding out which wire does what! However, it is important to know these details, and if something breaks it is crucial. Luckily the same rules govern every boat: thus it is the propellers which thrust the boat forward whether it is seventeen or seventy feet long; and diesel engines have basically the same needs, regardless of manufacturer. Although the details of an installation can vary widely, the basics regarding the way a system works remain constant, and it is those basics that we need to address when looking after the boat.

Narrow boats for leisure use have been built since the mid-sixties, and it is a tribute to their design and to the workmanship of their builders that virtually all these boats are still cruising along. It is also most definitely a glowing tribute to the care and maintenance lavished on them by their owners. A boat bought for a couple of thousand pounds in 1970 can be worth five times that now, but only if it is looked after.

The standards of boat construction have improved over the last thirty years. Steel plates have gradually become thicker, engines more powerful, and the rules governing gas and electrical systems increasingly complicated. The quality of boat building has seen a revolution, too. The first boats sported wooden roofs and plastic finishes on the walls, little or no insulation, and kitchen facilities that made a Boy Scouts' camp look luxurious. Today the cabins are lined with mahogany and cherry woods, central heating systems abound, and the beds have custom-made, fully sprung mattresses. Today's new boats are very much more expensive than their predecessors, but with a bit of work even an old boat can be upgraded to become really smart.

The first boat builders were untroubled by vast amounts of paperwork issuing from Brussels. Today, however, boat builders and owners alike have to be aware of safety regulations and EC directives. Gas and electrical systems represent a serious hazard in the shape of fire or electrocution, and there are a host of rules that really do need to be complied with. Although new safety standards are becoming mandatory for new boats built commercially, there is a compelling reason for every boat owner to ensure that his boat, however old, also meets them: a gas explosion in a narrow boat is a terrifying possibility, and regardless of the age of the boat, every step needs to be taken to prevent it. Some of the safety rules may appear to be somewhat 'over the top', but there are valid reasons behind them all. After all, even if there is only a one-in-a-million chance of an accident, would *you* want to be that one in a million?

Working on a boat has another advantage: not only will the work ensure a neat, tidy and efficient craft, but it usually brings you into contact with many other boaters. A general rule of thumb is one hour of actual work for every two spent gossiping about boats with other enthusiasts: handy tips for dealing with locks, horror stories about engines, what British Waterways are doing to Lock 44; boaters are a sociable lot, and there will almost always be a helping hand and plenty of advice while you are working on your boat.

As we have intimated already, unlike car drivers, boat owners are also fairly practical, and this must be the nature of the boating – anyone who can work out the complexities of cruising a boat on a waterway that was designed and built two hundred years ago has to be able to cope with most things. Changing a fuse is nothing if you have just worked through a staircase lock for the first time!

Boating is one of the few fields of modern technology that seems to ignore metric units almost completely, and only rarely do metres and kilograms crop up; the steel plate thickness is about the only thing regularly measured in metric, in millimetres. Boats continue to be measured in feet and inches, and tanks hold gallons. It can all be rather confusing to the novice, especially if he has only been taught about metric numbers. Ask most boaters what a 15-metre long boat looks like and you'll get a blank stare in return. Even the most modern diesel engines, awash with metric-sized bolts, are fitted with gearboxes that have AF, Whitworth, or UNC bolts. Besides, there are enough old engines about to keep metrification at bay for many years. No doubt the mandarins of Brussels are preparing some edict to rectify this problem, but as long as the idiosyncratic world of the waterways is alive, they don't stand a chance . . .

And so, on to the boat . . .

— 1 —

The Hull and Superstructure

Modern narrow boats are constructed from steel plates welded together to form a very strong and resilient hull and superstructure. Old narrow boats were made of wood or wrought-iron plates. Wood and wrought iron were superseded because steel is a much easier material to work, and although it rusts, it doesn't rot away like wood, and the rivets don't wear away and drop out as they do on wrought iron. The first modern steel hulls were made from 6mm (¼in) thick steel, but gradually the boat builders have increased the plate thicknesses so that a new boat today is quite likely to have a 10mm

Traditional boat, nearly a hundred years old and still carrying cargo.

Wooden BCN Tug being built.

thick bottom, 6mm sides and a 4mm cabin. A boat made with this amount of steel should last a very long time indeed. However, many boats are still made with only a 5mm thick hull and 3mm top, particularly at the cheaper end of the market. These do the job that they were built for, although they may not be around for your grandchildren to use. Boats of twenty and thirty years old are happily pottering along the cut with only 5mm-thick hull plates and none the worse for it. A boat's condition depends on how it is driven and cared for.

Steelwork Maintenance

The maintenance of a boat's steelwork can be divided into four areas: above and below the water, and inside and out. The topsides, above the water, are the easiest to inspect and can be observed every time you get on the boat. Rust is the biggest enemy of a steel boat, and a quick look over the paintwork will show up any tell-tale bubbles in the paint. The usual places where the rust starts are corners that hold water: the inside edge of the grab rail, the drain holes on the foredeck and especially on Cruiser-type sterns, all around the stern deck bearers.

Topsides

For each hole that is drilled through the steel, the paint film has been holed, making a starting-point for rust. Windows, ventilators,

Cruiser-style stern.

breather tubes and doors all give the water a chance to react with bare steel and start rusting. It always seems to be the most inaccessible places that rust first! Large flat expanses of steel are so much easier to prepare and paint, and are unlikely to corrode unless scratched.

Hull Sides

Below the water-line the exterior of the hull will be protected by the black paint customarily used for this purpose. It looks very smart when new, though after a few miles loses its gloss and gets covered in scratches and mud. Usually bitumen paint is used, because when it receives a knock or a bump the outer layer melts and smears rather than flakes off,

ensuring some degree of protection even after a scratch. A lot of new boats are painted with two-part epoxy paints instead of the old blacking; this is a very strong paint which will resist attack from solvents and abrasion.

The easiest part of this area of the boat to inspect is along the water-line; it is also where the paint is most prone to attack from diesel floating in the water, from weed growing on the hull, and of course from the mixture of air and water which starts off the rusting process. It is more difficult to have a look at the underneath. The principal points that get worn on the hull are the bends at the bows and stern, and to a lesser extent the bottom. Unlike sea-going boats, narrow boats will be scraping across mud and rubble in shallow water, crunching abandoned

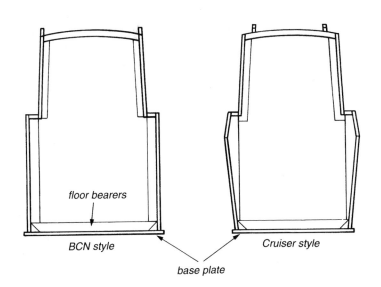
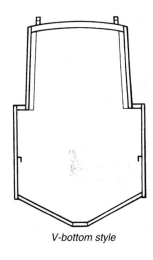

floor bearers

BCN style   Cruiser style   V-bottom style

base plate

Hull cross-sections.

shopping trolleys and generally roughing it. It is no wonder that the builders are using heavier and heavier grades of steel! A dry-docking session is the only way to inspect the bottom.

Interior

Inside the boat the steelwork can be hard to get at. There should be hatches in the floor to gain access to the bilges and ballast; open these up and move enough of the ballast to check the bottom. Ballast can cause its own problems. The most common materials are bricks and paving slabs which can act as powerful grinding tools unless there is a layer of protection between them and the steel; each time the boat goes bump they wear through the paint and steel a little more. Thus inside the bilges there should be a good thick layer of paint; it can be anything as long as it keeps the steel protected. A certain amount of water inevitably finds its way into the bilges – condensation, rain through an open door or leaky windows – and there will prob-

ably be a great deal of dirt down there, too, if it's an old boat. It is a difficult task to clean out a really filthy bilge, but it is important to keep it as clean as possible so as to keep rust at bay. A regular inspection and cleaning session once a year should maintain everything sufficiently.

The steel behind the cladding inside is usually completely inaccessible once the boat is built so it is of paramount importance that the builder applies a good paint or rust-prevention treatment before fitting the cabin lining. Condensation forms readily on cold steel and it can rust away unseen. It is possible to remedy a rusting section behind the cladding by using an injector spray, but it isn't very easy! Usually the problem just has to remain until the cladding can be stripped out and that section of the boat refitted.

Welds

It is also important to inspect the welds between the steel plates, particularly around the engine and bows. A boat is subjected to enormous stresses when it bangs into a lock, and no matter how carefully you drive, sooner or later you will fetch up against a lock cill with a thud hard enough to send the crockery flying; inevitably the welds around the bows are pushed and pulled as the boat resounds with the impact. It is quite rare for them to fail, but it is just as well to check them.

The engine bearers are subjected to lesser, but much more frequent vibration and stress: they absorb the energy from the engine, which often includes the thrust from the propeller, and transmit it to the hull, and the welds in this region *can* fail. Luckily it is usually a long process as a tiny crack gradually gets worse, and it isn't often that the crack will cause a hole in the hull. The weakest points, where the stresses do the most harm, are at the corners of the engine bearers. However, don't panic if you do find cracks in the welds, as a few minutes with an arc welder will sort the problem out. If you can't do the welding yourself, arrange for someone to do the job for you; it isn't expensive, and the problem is best tackled as soon as you detect it.

Painting and Rust Prevention

A good paint finish is the key to preventing rust. It can make the boat look very smart, too, although stopping rust is the first priority. Tidying up minor scratches is quick enough, just a matter of sanding down the affected area, applying an anti-rust primer like red oxide and repainting with the original colour. The problems really start when the paint is so old that it has faded away from its original colour, or there are so many scratches that hundreds of repairs are needed. Unless you want the boat to look mottled, it can be far less work to repaint the entire panel, or even the whole boat.

Painting steel need not be either difficult or costly. There are some very good marine-grade paints, like the two-part epoxy types and high gloss enamels. These paints are preferable because they give such a good finish, but they are not essential. To provide a good protection to the steel there must be a film of paint at least 100 microns thick. If the film is thinner it can crack as the steel expands and contracts with changing temperatures, and once cracked the water gets in. A normal coat of paint leaves a film 25 microns thick, so five coats of paint – one primer, two undercoats and two gloss finish – will adequately protect the steel. Although there are lots of boats that seem to be painted solely with red oxide primer, it is not a good policy to leave a boat like this as the primer does not prevent the water reaching the steel for any length of time.

Planning Paintwork

Painting a large area like a boat needs some planning. Ideally you need to sand off the old paint, prime the steel, and then apply the next four coats at twenty-four hour intervals, although the time between coats depends on the ambient temperature. Each coat has to dry off so that residual solvent is not trapped in the following coat; but the time lapse allowed mustn't be so long that the paint becomes too hard to bond with the next coat. If the time between coats exceeds about thirty-six hours then a rub down with fine sandpaper will be needed to key up the surface. Experience is the best guide as to how long to allow, but assuming the weather is a steady 60°F, twenty-four hours should be right.

This does presume at least five days of good weather, so you will need to watch the weather forecasts for a time of high pressure to get the best chance. The British climate is such an unpredictable beast that working in a covered dock is by far the best way to do the paintwork if you can't wait for the weather.

Painting in a covered dock to avoid the weather!

Preparation

The key to a successful paint finish on a boat is the preparation of the surface to be painted; the quality of the paint is of secondary importance. If the steel is badly prepared the paint will peel off whether it is super-expensive marine-grade gloss or a tin of tack from a boot fair. Rust needs to be thoroughly sanded away so there are no little specks left because these will start off the process again – rust has a greater volume than the steel that it replaces, and as it expands it cracks the paint, allowing more water in.

For larger areas of steel it is usually best to hire an industrial belt sander to scour off the old paint; little home-DIY sanders tend to give up when faced with a 70ft narrow boat!

If the rust has really penetrated into awkward corners a chemical rust treatment will neutralize it. These contain phosphoric acid in a gel: the acid is more reactive than steel and snatches the oxygen out of its chemical bond with the iron. Such treatments are very useful for getting into odd corners, but large-scale use of them is not such a good idea as the phosphorus will get into the water and cause pollution.

Once the surface is well prepared, the primer and new coats of paint can go on. Marine paint suppliers provide very full instructions for using their paints; ordinary undercoat and gloss can be applied using normal techniques, that is, brush or roller the paint on, allow to dry, and lightly sand down prior to the next coat if it has gone too hard.

Application Techniques

Applying the paint with a brush gives a very smooth finish whereas a roller tends to leave a slightly textured surface. The advantage of a roller is that it is much quicker, and although the film thickness is thinner than that of a brush-applied coat, extra coats can be applied quickly and easily. However, boats have more than their fair share of awkward corners which are tricky to reach with either a brush or an ordinary paint roller, so try the small 'radiator' rollers with long handles which can get the paint into most of them. It is only possible to spray thick paints like these if you have equipment that can cope, and it is not that common. The final coat will need to be 'laid off' by using gentle brush strokes all in the same direction.

Since a boat is so large you will need to plan out how you work along any one area because it is important that you always work from a wet edge: if you paint a piece and then leave it for a couple of hours, when you start painting again the join may crinkle up and spoil the gloss finish.

Lining Out

The final coat of gloss will make the boat look smart, and narrow boats also tend to have many lines of contrasting colours to enhance their appearance, as well as some spectacular artwork. The artwork is a specialist topic, though putting in the lines is simple enough; apply the lighter colour first, for instance if there is going to be a yellow line around a green superstructure, paint the yellow first and then use masking tape to give a precise edge to the green. Household masking tape is not much good for this since the paint can bleed under it, but sign-writer's edging tape

Traditional roof decoration and pigeon box.

is perfect because it is as thin as Sellotape but doesn't stick to the paint hard enough to pull it off when you remove it.

Deck Drainage

Getting the rainwater off a boat is important, and for a number of years boats have been made with self-draining decks. Traditional boats have such small and high stern decks that the water simply runs off the edge, but Cruiser, Semi-Trad and any boat with a large foredeck have to resort to more complicated techniques to deal with the water.

Foredecks are normally well above the water-line and the rain that falls into them is drained out via a pair of holes at the lowest points. These holes must not be allowed to become clogged up with leaves, because if they do, the water will collect and eventually seep over the threshold of the doors. The combination of this type of deck drainage and door height can cause some boats to run the risk of sinking. If the drainage holes are only a couple of inches above the water-line, and the front doors are only an inch or so above that, there is the risk that the threshold of the doors could be pushed below the water-line. All it takes is a full water tank and a half-a-dozen people sitting on the bows, and in comes the water. The threshold of the doors should be 10in (25cm) above the water-line.

The stern deck of Cruisers and Semi-Trad boats is usually supported by a combination of fixed and movable steel channels, and the rainwater runs off the deck boards into these channels and then out through the hull sides. The channels need to be kept clean as it doesn't take many leaves to obstruct them.

A lot of older boats do not have a self-draining deck so the rainwater collects in the bilges and has to be pumped out every so often. This design is a nuisance. If the boat has to be left unattended for a long time it must have a cover put over the deck, and an automatic bilge pump fitted.

Engine Bilges

This has to be the messiest place on any boat, apart from the waste-holding tanks – leaves, oil, rainwater and the occasional dead frog all end up in here. But cleanliness is important, since it is all too easy to drop some small component of the engine in here, never to be seen again. The engine should have an oil drip tray to prevent oil contaminating the bilge and consequently the canal water. If the area has become seriously contaminated because of an oil leak, there are some environmentally friendly degreasants available which will break up the oil into more harmless compounds.

Blacking the Hull and Dry Docking

A quick lick of black bitumen above the water-line really perks up the appearance of a boat in the spring. Otherwise a boat will need to be dry docked about once every five years, and that is the opportunity to clean it up really thoroughly and paint it below the water-line.

The Dry Dock

The dry dock will need to be booked well in advance, as there can be a long waiting list for docks in popular parts of the system. The procedure is simplicity itself; the boat cruises into the dock, just like a lock, and the water is let out; this allows the boat to rest on stocks set into the floor of the dock. Simplicity for flat-bottomed boats, anyway – if your boat is a Springer or any make with a V-bottom, chocks will need to be placed on the sides to prevent it tipping to one side.

Cranes

If there is no dry dock close to you, or you need to work on the boat's hull in a hurry and

Early 'Springer' out for inspection.

they can't fit you in, all is not lost. Many boats are lifted out of the water with a crane and placed on a hard standing area. This is quite an expensive performance, since twenty-five ton cranes cost a lot of money; they charge by the hour, and it is usual to book a crane twice, once to lift the boat out, and then a second visit to put it back in the water. Advance planning is helpful because yours might not be the only boat needing to be craned in and out, and sharing the cost will reduce the bill dramatically.

Finally, let me reassure you: a narrow boat swinging in the air looks very dramatic, but trust the crane driver – they do this quite often, and I have never yet heard of a boat being dropped!

Side Slips

Long before cranes were invented, an alternative to dry docking was the side slipway, particularly for boats being built. This is really just a very wide (70ft/21m) slipway with greased rails; the boat is winched sideways up the slip, worked on, and shoved back down. The drawback is that only one boat can use it at a time. If you ever get the chance to watch a new boat being launched off a side slip, go and see it. The boat is jacked up onto special rocking stocks, known as Boss stocks; at the crucial moment it is allowed to tilt, then it slides onto the greased rails and rushes sideways down into the water. The splash is memorable!

A side launch of a replica Thames barge.

Working on the Hull

Once the boat is in the dry dock, time is of the essence since there is usually a queue of boats waiting to get in and the owner may well be charging by the day. Some dry docks won't allow sand- or grit-blasting to take place in their dock as the grit silts up the dock; however, most will, because it is a very quick way of removing all the old paint and dirt from the hull sides. The blasting is usually done by contractors who whisk round the boat with their equipment and in a couple of hours the steelwork looks like new – though the inside of the boat may not! The process creates dust in vast quantities – putting tape over every hatch and window, ventilator and breather tube will help keep it out.

Once the contractors are out of the way you can start applying the paint, as many coats as time allows – after all, it has to last till the next dry docking; five coats should be sufficient. If the weather is cold the bitumen can be warmed up by standing the tin in a bucket of hot water. Do *not* stick a blow lamp on to the tin, and try not to have any welding going on whilst the paint is wet because it is possible to set wet bitumen paint on fire.

If you are feeling really enthusiastic you can even paint underneath the boat, but very few people bother with this. The underside of the hull rarely grows weed, or even rusts, since it is so deep in the water that light and oxygen don't reach it. A constant diet of shopping trolleys and bricks tends to keep it pretty clean, too.

A dry dock.

Other Work

Dry docking allows other activities as well. For example, it is a very good opportunity for a surveyor to look at the boat should your insurance company need a survey. Boats over twenty years old worry insurance companies, and they frequently insist on a full survey before providing cover. The surveyor has a gadget called an ultrasonic thickness tester which will measure the thickness of the steel without having to drill holes in it. The old-fashioned way was to belt the steel with a ball pein hammer; if it went right through then the steel wasn't thick enough. However, ultrasonic gadgets don't work on wrought iron because of its laminated internal structure, so the hammer has not passed into history yet.

Sacrificial Anodes

Anodes are an important part of the battle against corrosion: they are chunks of metal bolted or welded onto the hull below the water-line, made of a metal with a higher electrochemical value than steel, which in ordinary language means that they corrode more quickly. A boat hull sitting in the water is a bit like a battery, and a tiny voltage is formed between the prop and steel; a process not unlike electroplating starts up and the steel is leached away. By adding the anodes into the circuit, the anodes corrode first, and after a few years will need to be replaced with fresh ones; exactly how long is determined by the quality of the water the boat lives in. When a boat is in dry dock it is a straightforward task to replace them. Never paint over them, as this would insulate them from the water and defeat the object. A 50ft boat will usually have four anodes, two at each end, and they are best sited where they are unlikely to get rubbed away in the swim. Full-length boats really need six, but the only way to site a pair in the middle is inside a recess in the hull, and few boat builders provide these. If you are using weld on anodes, double check that there is nothing inflammable on the other side of the steel; floor bearers or cladding can ignite on contact with the hot metal.

Improvements to the Stern Gear

Dry docking provides opportunities for improvements and other maintenance. A close inspection of the propeller is a good idea: has it become worn or cracked? Is it the right size? If a boat has had a new engine and gearbox fitted, it may not be. If the boat seems to be using a lot of fuel, or to be underpowered, a new prop may help; the prop size will be stamped on the centre boss (although it may be illegible after a few years!). Dry docking provides the chance to fit an item called a 'Stripper' – a pair of blades, one on the prop, and one on the stern tube – which effectively chops up any rope that gets caught in the prop blades before it does any serious damage.

The propeller shaft and bearings can be checked for damage, too. The shaft can be bent, and the end bearing of the stern tube

The propeller size is crucial to achieve the correct engine performance.

A 1930s wrought-iron motor-boat stern.

stern tube needs to be checked. The packing is normally slightly compressed by tightening up the end plate once a year, and it is prevented from wearing away by forcing grease from the stern tube greaser into the gland. This keeps the water out and lubricates the shaft. After some years the packing will wear away altogether, and although it can be changed with the boat in the water, the process is simpler whilst you are in the dry dock.

Weed Hatches

Weed hatches are rarely used, or even thought about, until a mattress wraps itself around the prop; then you may find that the boat builder obviously thought you had arms one inch wide and four feet long, with several more elbows than normal. Some builders put in ludicrously small hatches which simply don't do the job; if so, the inferior hatch can be cut out whilst the boat is in dock and a new, decent-sized one put in. If you can get both hands down the hatch onto the propeller and still wrestle hard with a tyre, then it's big enough; if you can't, the thing is useless.

If the hatch *is* big enough, remember to check that the cleaning and painting process has reached all the way up it, past the baffle. The seal at the top may need renewing, too: this is a self-adhesive foam tape which makes a watertight seal as it is compressed. If the seal breaks down, the water pressure from the propeller will squirt through the gap and gradually fill the bilges. The classic way for narrow boats to sink is because the weed hatch has not been bolted down tight enough. Some builders incorporate a switch on the hatch top to sound an alarm if it isn't closed down tight, and it might be a good idea to fit one yourself.

can wear away, allowing the shaft to rattle sideways; in both cases the remedy is replacement. If the prop-shaft has been bent it will probably have caused excess wear on the stern tube. Stern tubes come in two types, weld-in or bolt-in: the latter can be changed very simply, the former will need an engineer. In either case the alignment of the shaft and engine will need to be checked and probably corrected afterwards.

The rudder bearings can also be inspected. Although they usually last for decades, some cheaper makes of boat have extremely simple bearings, just a short bit of pipe welded to the skeg, and this can wear away. However, because it is so simple it is easy to replace.

The packing gland at the inboard end of the

Major Works

Dry docking also provides the place to carry

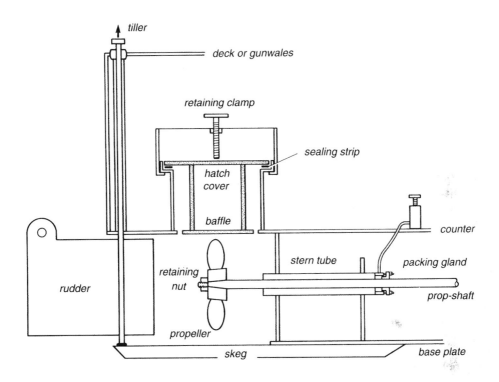

The weed hatch.

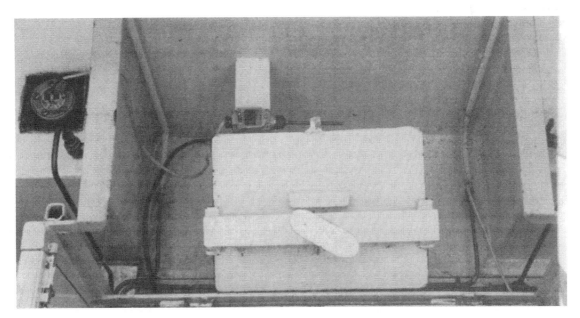

A quick-release weed hatch, with an alarm switch fitted.

Rebottoming an old boat.

out the most dramatic of work: rebottoming and stretching, both fairly major events in a boat's life, and both of them tasks for professionals only. Rebottoming involves cutting the old bottom off, and welding an entire new one on; stretching is when the boat is cut in half, the two ends separated and a new section placed in between. Both processes involve some heavy lifting and cutting gear, and need to be planned by the contractor and the boat owner well in advance.

Welding

For boats that are very old and getting a touch thin in places, dry docking provides the chance to weld new pieces in place. If you are a good welder it is quite feasible to do this

yourself, otherwise get a professional to do the job. The problem with cutting and fitting new steel into place is that often there is a lot of woodwork just behind it, which could be set on fire. All inflammable material needs to be removed from the work area. The areas that usually need this kind of treatment are the ends of the bow and stern swims, since they are the most exposed parts of the hull. In fact it is worth welding on some extra rubbing strakes whilst you're about it – but do be careful not to make the boat any wider than 7ft or you'll be getting wedged in thin locks!

The steelwork of a boat can probably last for ever; rather like an old broom that has had four new heads and three handles. It is beyond the scope of this book to discuss welding skills, but it is very useful to know how to do it, and it can be picked up quite quickly. Most Further Education colleges run evening classes, and the basics can be gleaned from the instruction book that comes with a welder. The British Oxygen Company also runs instruction courses for novices at their regional centres. Otherwise a bit of common sense and a great deal of practice are all that is required.

Boats are normally welded with an electric arc, but they can be done with MIG or TIG or even the good old-fashioned oxy-acetylene – and if someone tells you that you can't weld 10mm-thick steel with oxy-acetylene, just tell them that they mean *they* can't. A good welder can use any method to achieve a good weld, if he has the right tools and knows what he is doing.

Weatherproofing and Security

Windows, Doors and Leaks

It is a rare event for boats to leak from the bottom, but unfortunately leaks through the windows and doors are much more common. Each hole in the superstructure – ventilators, windows, doors, chimneys and flues – represents a route for rainwater to enter the boat, water which then proceeds to ruin the woodwork and furnishings, leaving the boat with a musty smell and generally spoiling anything it touches. And the trouble with leaks is that it can be the very devil to find where they come from.

The most common places for leaks to start are where wood has been screwed to the steel. Wooden handrails used to be common on boats, held in place by a screw from the inside of the cabin. Wood shrinks as it dries and expands in the wet, and thus the wood in the rails would successfully break up any sealant used around the screw. The screws themselves rust away, too; at first just a little water finds its way through, causing the screws to

rust further, and gradually the process accelerates until rusty stains appear inside the boat, and eventually the handrail falls off the boat. Of course it is most likely to come off when you pull on it, which will be the time you most need it, so to avoid an unnecessary swim in the cut, it is a problem that needs to be tackled promptly. The best solution is to remove the wooden handrail, clean out all the screw holes and plug them with fibreglass filler, and weld a steel handrail in place.

Any wood attached to steel is suspect – the traditional cants at the bows, doorways and hatches are all places where leaks are common. Wood has different characteristics to steel, and getting a good permanent bond between the two is virtually impossible. Silicon sealant has to be the best compromise available, as it remains pliable and thus takes up the differing expansion rates.

Ventilators are not usually a problem because they are normally sited on the highest part of the roof and so the water can always run away from them. Flues and chimneys are another matter, though, as these are often on the roof edge, exactly the point to which the rain runs. Silicon sealant can cope with the heat from a small water heater, and can thus be used to seal a brass flue cover, but chimneys have to be sealed down with a heat-resistant gasket compound; they are prone to leakage because the thermal expansion of the chimney collar is greater than the roof, which breaks down the seal. They also have an annoying tendency to dribble coal tar out onto the roof.

Doors are not too much of a problem. On a well-made boat the sides contain a channel which catches any wind-blown water and drains it out at the bottom. If you have a cheaper boat this may not be the case so that water drips onto the steps; it is worth taking measures to remedy this by glueing hardwood or plastic battens to the sides and doorstep – a good filler adhesive will make the bond very strong and waterproof, too.

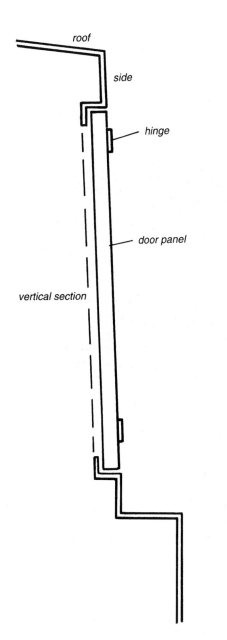

roof

side

hinge

door panel

vertical section

Security

Doors have to keep out more than the weather: they must also protect against the unscrupulous rogues who break into boats and steal whatever they can find. Flimsy wooden doors are not really sufficient and if your boat has these, it is worth thinking seriously about replacing them with steel.

Possibly worse than human intruders are mink, which can squeeze through a remarkably small gap and will happily make an unattended boat their winter quarters. The resulting mess of ransacked cupboards and the remnants of a month's fish dinners has to be seen to be believed. The doors therefore need to be a good fit; also burglar alarms may be advisable in some areas (see Chapter 3 concerning electrical appliances).

Window Leaks

Windows do have a tendency to leak: not only is there the large hole to take the frame, but dozens of little ones for the screws. A new window has a sealing strip of rubber which compresses as the window frame is screwed down; ten years later this strip is quite likely to have failed, allowing the wet to get in. Other older types of window didn't even have this, and were bedded into place with a mastic sealant; the mastic dries up and cracks, and again in comes the rain. Unfortunately the mastic doesn't dry up completely, but always leaves enough of itself pliable to create a hideous mess when you come to replace it.

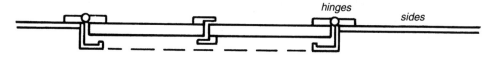

hinges

sides

Door drainage and draught proofing.

Windows can be fastened with screws, bolts or blind pop rivets.

The best way to cure a leaky window is to unscrew it from the boat, remove the old sealing strip or mastic, and put in a new neoprene strip (available from the window manufacturers). If only life were so simple, but not all boats have their windows screwed directly to the steel: a lot have the screws going through a hole into the wooden frame behind the steel. That isn't a problem if the frame is fixed in place by the internal linings, but be careful: some boat builders would use the window frame to support the cabin lining, rather than weld tags to the inside of the steel. The result of this neat little bit of planning is that if you remove the windows, the cabin lining falls to the floor.

If the window is fixed to an uneven surface the sealing strip may not be able to take up all the gap. Silicon sealant from a gun dispenser is the quickest and simplest way around this, though beware – silicon sealants are very sticky when first exposed to the air and will stick to just about anything; the user's fingers are a favourite, followed by everything he touches. As the sealant cures it releases acetic acid gas (that's the vinegar smell associated with it), and this gas can lightly corrode metals; if you work carelessly you will find black finger-prints everywhere the following day!

To get the best from the sealant when replacing the window frame, apply a bead of it around the window aperture where the edge of the aluminium frame covers it, being especially careful to cover the screw holes. Lightly insert the window frame until it is just starting to squeeze the sealant out of the gap, and insert all the screws. When the screws are tightened the sealant will be exuded out of the gap as it closes, and try to smear everything in sight. To prevent this happening take a mist sprayer – the sort for keeping house plants damp – and spray water very lightly all over the area. Tighten up the screws being careful not to touch the exuding sealant. A day later the surplus hardened sealer can be trimmed off with a razor blade, and the job will look as smart as any professional could achieve.

Replacing Glass

Narrow boat windows are made with toughened glass. This takes a lot to break, but lock balance beams do seem to have a way of swinging into the side of a boat and smashing the windows. As long as the windows are made by one of the main manufacturers this need not be a major catastrophe because they keep a stock of replacement glass for all their common sizes; even if it is an unusual size they will be able to get a new piece toughened faster than an ordinary glazier. You can either take the frame apart and replace the glass with its rubber seal yourself, or take the whole frame to them to do.

A non-standard window can be replaced in much the same way, except that it may take a couple of weeks for the replacement glass to be toughened. Toughening is a heat-treatment process which turns ordinary glass into something stronger and harder; it is rather like case hardening steel. The companies that do the work have a queue of window panes waiting to go on their process line; however, the boat window makers are regular customers, with more clout than the average High Street glazier.

Wooden and Glassfibre Superstructures

Not all boats have steel superstructures. Early cruising boats were quite often working boats converted to leisure use by the simple expedient of building a shed over the hold. The first purpose-built pleasure craft followed this example, and the cabin top was an optional extra. It might seem a bit odd these days, but it did allow people to get their own steel hull at a much reduced price, and build the cabin when they could afford it.

Plywood is a cheap and versatile material, but it doesn't last for any great time and in a lot of the early boats built with wooden cabins these are now falling to bits. The normal practice was to build a hardwood frame for

A BCN Tug in dock for repairs.

the superstructure, and screw plywood sheets to this. The joints were waterproofed with mastic tape and the whole liberally painted to keep out the weather. The wooden surface requires substantially more maintenance than a steel one. The wood needs to be well painted every couple of years, and at least once a decade the old paint will need to be burnt off, the wood treated with a preservative, and a new paint finish applied.

The plywood eventually goes soft and succumbs to wet rot. However, if the timber frames are still intact there is little reason why the sheets should not be replaced when they go. Unfortunately the frames do have a tendency to rot where they are bolted to the steel, and when this happens the time has come to think about removing the cabin and having a steel top welded on. Although the cabin roof appears to be there simply and solely to keep out the rain, it in fact also has to act as launch and landing pad for the crew as they work the locks, and this puts quite a strain on its structure.

Glassfibre is a far more resilient material. Unless it is smashed by a close encounter with a bridge, or a very heavy member of the crew jumps on it from a great height, it should last indefinitely. It can be painted using a proprietary paint system, and it can also be repaired fairly easily if it suffers minor damage, in much the same way as a fibreglass Cruiser.

The points to watch with glassfibre tops are the places where the glass and steel join. This join can either be a direct chemical bond between the fibre and steel or, more usually, with bolts; whichever it is, this union can be weakened by years of bumps and rust. Windows can also be a problem with older boats as the frames tend to work loose, gradually shedding all the screws. This indicates that the holes have probably worn out, and before the frames are screwed back into place, each hole will need a dab of fibreglass filler.

Inside the boat there will be support struts bonded into the material to strengthen the roof and sides. These struts were originally pieces of softwood glassed into place. On some boats woodrot has completely destroyed them and the roof has become seriously weakened as a result. If this is happening on your boat there are two alternatives: new struts can be stuck to the glassfibre alongside the old ones, or you can start saving for a steel cabin!

When a wooden or GRP cabin comes to the end of its useful life and the expense of a steel cabin looks inevitable, do make sure that the hull underneath is still strong enough to make the expense worthwhile. If the boat has recorded a high mileage the plates may be worn very thin, and the expense of a complete overhaul may be more than the value of the boat. Boats of this age can cost a lot more than they are worth to keep in good order, much like an old car.

Cleaning the Boat

It is important to keep the boat clean because mud soon finds its way all over the roof and sides, forming an effective grinding paste which ruins the paintwork; even the rain contains fine particles of soot and grime which spoil the boat's appearance. Thus a good wash down will do wonders for the longevity of the paintwork – though it isn't always so good for the fish in the water. There are several brands of ecologically friendly cleaners available these days, and they will help keep the canal water clean, too. Yes, I know it looks pretty murky stuff, but we don't want it to get any worse!

Summary

The maintenance of a boat's structure is the key to its long life, its pleasing appearance and its value as an investment. The work, for

Inside a dry dock.

work it is, need not be done in huge bursts of activity: a little observation and remedial action whenever you are on board will save a lot of worry and expense later on. A long-term plan is important to ensure that the major events in a boat's life are taken care of. Dry docking is one, but it need only happen once every five years as long as all the important repairs are carried out at that time. Such an overall plan will help to ensure that the main-

tenance of the boat is quite as good as that given by any professional boat builder; and a strategy of regular care will also help you carry out each task in an orderly way, thus achieving a high quality result. If you leave a boat's maintenance until something breaks, the inevitable result will be a hurried bodge, a last-minute attempt to salvage something from a holiday that has turned from a pleasant cruise into a succession of breakdowns.

Basic Engine Maintenance and Servicing

Narrow boat transmission systems are simple enough in principle. A diesel engine converts the chemical energy in the fuel into a mechanical rotary force, the gearbox adjusts this to the desired direction of rotation, the reduction ratio matches the revolutions per minute of the engine to that needed by the propeller, and the propeller converts the rotary force to that of thrust. The thrust is then transmitted back up the prop-shaft and through to the hull. It's so simple that unless the system is badly installed, there isn't much to go wrong.

The care of the engine is in two parts, servicing and repairs. If it isn't broken, *don't fix it*. More engines end up at the scrapyard because of well-intentioned tinkering than ever wear out.

Modern diesels are sophisticated machines, needing very little in the way of servicing. However, to give their best they need a certain amount of understanding. A diesel is a compression ignition motor; unlike a petrol engine which ignites the fuel/air mix with a spark, the diesel relies on

the high temperature generated by the immense compression of the air. The fuel is injected just before maximum compression, explodes and releases its energy. In that one sentence lies the greatest weakness of the engine, the injection.

The injectors have to squirt liquid fuel into a chamber, turning it into a mist spray,

---

Propeller pitch guide

Modern engine with 3:1 gearbox

| Prop Diam. (in) | Boat length | | | | | |
	20ft	30ft	40ft	50ft	60ft	70ft
16	8	10	12	–	–	–
18	–	10	12	14	16	–
20	–	–	12	14	16	18
22	–	–	12	14	16	18
24	–	–	–	16	18	20

Vintage Engine with 2:1 gear box

| Prop Diam. (in) | Boat length | | | | | |
	20ft	30ft	40ft	50ft	60ft	70ft
16	10	12	14	–	–	–
18	–	12	14	16	–	–
20	–	–	14	16	18	–
22	–	–	–	16	18	20
24	–	–	–	18	20	22

This is a very approximate guide because every boat has a different combination of engine, gearbox and propeller

---

Engine power to boat length ratio

Length (ft)	20	30	40	50	60	70
Engine horsepower at prop shaft	5	10	15	20	25	30

Less power is needed for Semi-V hulls, more for deeper than average draught hulls.

The popular BMC 1.5 litre engine.

Stern tube greaser.

while the pressure inside is already fifteen or twenty times that of the outside air. The slightest trace of dirt in the fuel can block the injector, and anything less than exactly the right amount of fuel leads to a loss of power. Thus care for the engine starts with a constant regard for the cleanliness of the fuel. Every time the tank is filled, take care not to allow water or dirt to drop in the tank. If you have a dipstick to measure the fuel level, ensure that it is always clean.

Care of the Engine

There are checks that can be made daily to keep the engine in good order. The lubricat-ing oil will need to be monitored, as will the stern tube greaser. The fan belt tension can slacken off and slow the charging rate for the batteries without making the charging light come on; each time you intend to start the motor have a quick look at it – this might seem a chore, but it will give you advance warning of any problems. The fuel pipes need to be a good fit. As they get older they can corrode and either dribble diesel out, or let air in; the former leaves you with stinking bilges, and both will diminish the performance of the engine.

The coolant hoses also suffer with age and eventually perish, so a little leak is generally advance notice that a spare pipe is needed; little leaks grow up to be major ones, resulting in loss of the coolant and an overheating

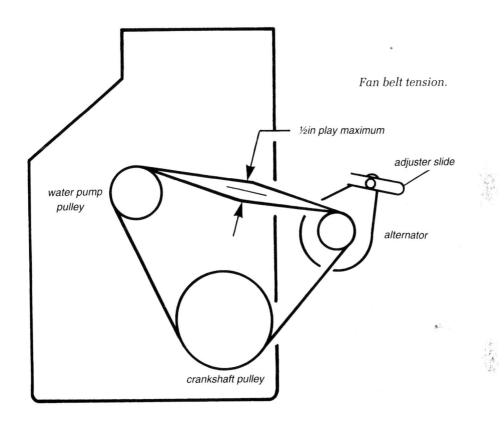

Fan belt tension.

½in play maximum

adjuster slide

water pump
pulley

alternator

crankshaft pulley

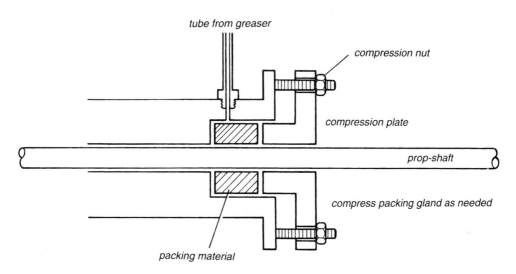

tube from greaser

compression nut

compression plate

prop-shaft

compress packing gland as needed

packing material

Packing gland.

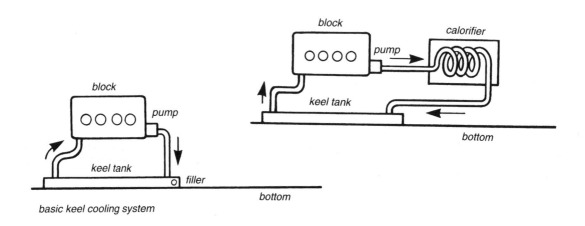

basic keel cooling system

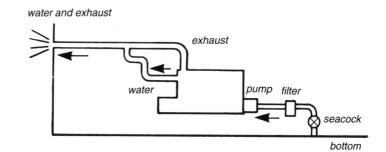

Engine cooling system.

engine. A look at the other connections between the boat and motor is also a good idea; they are all subject to vibration as the motor shakes in relation to the hull. The control cables should look well greased and unfrayed; the silencer can develop cracks, particularly in the flexible section; other weak points to check are the engine mounting bolts and the flexible connector on the prop-shaft. Just a quick look each day – each of these parts gets plenty of thorough attention during a service, but a glance can spot the unexpected fault before it becomes a catastrophe.

Engines that are cooled using canal water often suffer from a clogged inlet filter and this needs to be inspected every day, more often if there is a lot of weed or debris in the water. A constant watch on the temperature gauge should be second nature to anyone with this type of engine cooling system. Another of its potentially fatal drawbacks is that if the pipes fracture due to vibration, frost or just old age, the boat could be in danger of sinking; sea cocks must therefore be fitted to any water inlet below the water-line, and these must be checked and kept in good order constantly. Each winter the engine will need to be drained down fully to prevent frost damaging the engine (there will be instructions for this in the engine manual).

Most boats nowadays are fitted with a keel

Cooling water intake; note the seacock and large filter.

space at the top will allow water vapour into the tank, which can contaminate the fuel.

The daily care of the engine may seem a little onerous, but it quickly becomes second nature. Besides, the consequences of engine failure can be serious, particularly on river navigations. You might start the day's cruising on a gentle little canal but just hours later you may find yourself battling against the current on a river, and the nagging doubts caused by the clanks and steam issuing from the engine compartment won't enhance your pleasure.

Safety

Before doing anything with the engine it is important to ensure that it cannot be started inadvertently. This is a particular danger for traditional boats with an engine room, because it is quite possible for someone to fiddle with the ignition switch not realizing that someone else is working on the motor; if the engine was to fire the results could be fatal. Always turn off the electrical isolator switch and decompress the engine when working on the moving parts.

Some faults on a diesel engine can cause it to 'run away', that is, it decides to run full tilt and the revs climb steadily towards, and even past the red line. Twiddling the stop control has no effect and most people's instinct is to run for it! However, if an engine does this and will not respond to the stop control, it can be stopped by turning off the fuel tap to prevent further fuel getting to the engine, or blocking the air filter to stop air entering the cylinder and firing the diesel. Don't block the air filter with your hand, use a large rag.

Main Service

Once a year, or after every hundred hours of use, the engine will need a service; even if the boat has only been used a couple of days in the year it is worth doing the full service.

cooling tank: this enables the engine to lose its surplus heat through the hull, or even into a hot water cylinder. The great advantage of this system is that the same coolant is constantly recycled, and can have corrosion inhibitors and antifreeze added; and it doesn't try to pump plastic bags through the engine, either!

The fuel filter will need to be checked regularly; ideally an engine will have a water separator before the main filter. Drain off any accumulated water before starting a holiday, and always check it about once a month. The filter should be good for a year, depending on how many hours the engine is used. It is a good idea to keep the tank full because the air

The ventilation of traditional engine 'oles is important.

Lister FR3 in a traditional engine 'ole.

Visual Inspection

It is important to check the engine mounting bolts, fuel and exhaust pipes, fan belt tension, air filter and control cables before running up the engine; if you try to check these when the engine has got hot, you will probably burn your arms.

Engine Alignment

The engine mounting bolts are extremely important. Most modern engine installations take the thrust of the propeller through the gearbox and transmit it to the hull through the engine mounts. This saves on the cost of a plumber block, a thrust-absorbing bearing on the prop-shaft, but it puts a stress on the engine casing. To check the mounts use two spanners, one above and one below the engine lug; if you only tighten the top one down, the engine alignment will be disturbed: by tightening one spanner against the

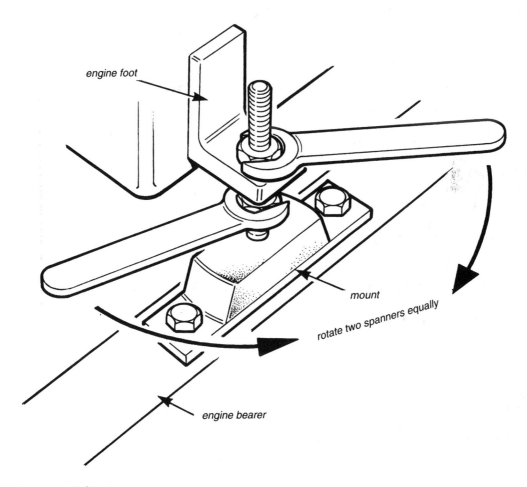

Engine mount tightening.

other with equal force the lug will remain in situ.

The engine alignment is a crucial part of the system when the thrust is transmitted up the prop-shaft and through the engine mounts to the hull structure. A good, although rough guide as to how accurate it is, is to check the friction between the propeller and the gearbox. This is done by turning off the isolator switches so the engine cannot be started, reaching down through the weed hatch and with the gearbox in neutral, turning the prop by hand. If the propeller turns

easily then the system should be lined up; if it takes a lot of effort, or isn't even possible, then the engine is probably out of line. 'Easily' means freely rotating without any stiff points in the circle. It always takes a certain amount of effort to get it moving – you won't do it with one finger – but you shouldn't have to exert so much effort that you graze your skin.

If the engine has become misaligned the first thing to try and establish is why it happened. A serious bang on the prop can loosen the bolts, and once loose the nuts will work

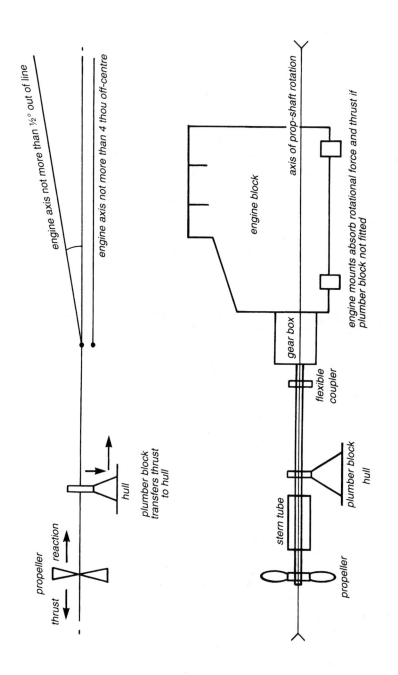

engine axis not more than ½° out of line

engine axis not more than 4 thou off-centre

axis of prop-shaft rotation

engine block

engine mounts absorb rotational force and thrust if
plumber block not fitted

gear box

flexible
coupler

plumber block
transfers thrust
to hull

hull

propeller

reaction

thrust

plumber block

hull

stern tube

propeller

Engine alignment for Cruiser-style transmission.

free. A brand-new engine will invariably work its engine mounts loose, no matter how tightly you do them up at first. The rubber inside flexible mounts can perish or come unstuck from the metal housing. If the mounts have failed, then new ones are a matter of urgency since the stresses on the engine's own feet are consequently increased and they can fracture.

A simple method to realign the engine is to construct a tripod above the engine block and use an engine hoist to suspend the motor in exactly the right place while the engine mounting nuts are loose. A lot of jiggling about can then take place until the motor is lined up with the prop-shaft coupler. This will need to be within $^4/_{1000}$in sideways and half a degree lengthways if you are using a plastic coupler; couplers which look like a

rubber-filled cup are slightly more forgiving about this tolerance. Whichever sort you use, bear in mind that the further away from exact alignment the motor and prop-shaft are, the less efficient the propulsion system will be. The coupler's life, and that of the gearbox, will also be shortened. When the engine is correctly positioned the nuts on the engine mounts can be tightened up.

The old working boats had the engine sitting in a cabin all on its own. The inboard end of the prop-shaft had a plumber block which transmitted the thrust to the hull, and the rotary force was carried along another prop-shaft from the engine. This main shaft was often fitted with two universal joints to allow a bend in the transmission line. Many boats are still built with this type of system. A traditional engine, with all its polished

'Uniflex' coupler, of the sort that resembles a rubber-filled cup.

pipework and its gentle low revving sound, is one of the beauties of canal boats, bringing to mind the days when British-built engines powered an empire and each one was a testament to the quality of our engineers. Those days haven't really passed, but it seems that the canals are one of the few places left where people can still take pride in a finely built engine. The drawback is that on top of the ordinary maintenance, it is essential to spend several hours metal-polishing.

The basic care of a traditional engine is just the same. The plumber block will need a greasing, as will the universal joints and the throttle wheel and gear rod bearings. This layout enables the engine to be mounted in a wider range of positions. It also removes the main propulsion thrust from the engine block, giving a much longer life for the engine mounts. The only critical alignment is that of the plumber block, which is usually mounted on such a solid piece of steel that it doesn't

Aqua-drive bearing and a stern tube.

move. It the prop hits something hard, either the prop or the thing will break!

Running Inspection

An engine will reveal a lot by the way it sounds. As it warms, the oil pressure should stabilize and the noise become smoother – cold engines always sound rough. The running temperature of a diesel engine should be about 80° C on the engine block: above this, and the engine's gaskets will have a short life; below it, and the cylinders will be prone to carbon deposits. Normally it should take no more than fifteen minutes to reach this temperature – any longer and the thermostat is suspect.

An engine in good condition will purr along without any hard knocking sounds or noticeable exhaust fumes. Clouds of white smoke will indicate faulty injectors, and black smoke a poorly adjusted injector pump. Practically speaking, any fault of this nature requires professional attention. Hard knocking sounds from inside the block can be caused by various bearings wearing out, the big end and little ends being the first to go usually followed by the crankshaft bearings. To get at these involves stripping the engine to bits. If you are a diesel engine mechanic it's no problem; if you are not, don't try it!

The Gearbox

The gearbox is a delicate piece of engineering, despite the pummelling it has to withstand. There is a wide variety of types used, so as regards maintenance it is difficult to suggest anything other than to read the instruction manual and follow that. The weak points tend to be the coolant pipes and the coupling to the prop-shaft. Different engineers will swear that one make is better than another, that such-and-such a make

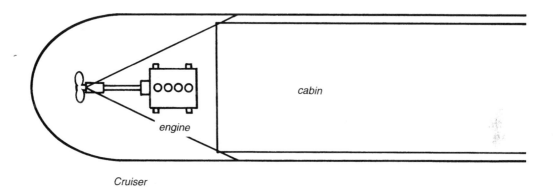

Cruiser

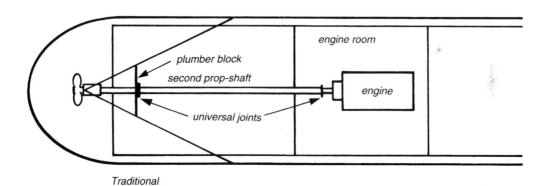

Traditional

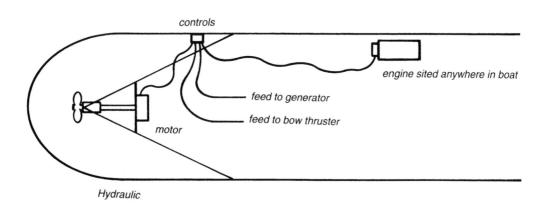

Hydraulic

Engine layouts.

always fails, that the ratios aren't what they should be. Don't listen, modern gearboxes will withstand an awful lot of abuse before packing up. The alignment of the prop-shaft into them determines their life; if they have to take much sideways force, they will all eventually fail.

The control cables to the throttle and gearbox must also be greased; they can be unhooked from the single lever control and held vertically whilst oil is dribbled down them. The control lever will benefit from a splodge of grease on its movement, too.

Care of the Exhaust System

The exhaust pipe is in constant vibration when the engine is running and is therefore prone to fracture. A wet exhaust system, which takes canal water through the engine and expels it with the exhaust gasses, shows up any fractures readily because there is water everywhere! A dry exhaust, however, will be lagged with insulating cloth and can quietly emit poisonous gas through a fracture with no outward signs of trouble; it is important therefore to unwind the lagging and look for faults. Flexible lengths of pipe come in two sorts: the best have the bellows fabricated out of solid steel, the other is a type of wound coil; the latter rusts quite quickly and ceases to be flexible after only a few years. The silencer should be good for many years, although it may eventually clog up with soot. A new silencer can be obtained from a chandler and fitted easily enough; they usually have threaded ends.

Drive Belt

The belt driving the alternator (and often the cooling water pump) is subjected to more rigorous use in a narrow boat than in a car or lorry. Boats are fitted with a host of electrical appliances, all of which are ultimately driven by the alternator, and inevitably this places a strain on the belt, causing it to stretch and slacken off. It should have about half an inch play on its longest side; this play will increase with age, and then it is best to re-tension the belt by adjusting the alternator position. As a belt gets older it will also start to give off a black dust; if this is visible it's time to get a spare. Further, if there are patches on the belt where the material is starting to break down, it's time to fit the spare and get another in stock.

The Water Pump

The water pump is a crucial element of a boat's cooling system driven from the drive belt. Most engines use an impeller-type

Normal belt-driven water pump and alternator.

pump which will need to be examined for wear; the rubber impellers go hard and brittle with age, so keeping a spare impeller and gasket on board is always a good idea. This check will involve losing some of the coolant, so don't forget to check the level and top it up afterwards. Some water pumps have their own little greaser, just like the stern tube one only smaller. This will need to be kept full of waterproof grease, and given a turn regularly to keep the water pump working efficiently.

Cooling System

The coolant pipes will want a close inspection, as the rubber can perish. If it looks old and leaves a black dust on your hand when touched, at least make sure you have a spare, if not actually replace the pipe. The coolant in a keel-cooled engine is a mixture of water and antifreeze. Commercial antifreeze mixture contains a corrosion inhibitor as well as ethylene glycol antifreeze; the glycol will go on working for years, but the corrosion inhibitors get used up in about three so it makes good sense to replace the coolant after this interval. A half-and-half mixture of water and antifreeze will protect the engine to −10° C, which should cover most winters.

Alternator and Split Charge Testing

If you have a voltmeter then it is easy enough to check the charging circuit of the alternator. When the engine is off, the voltage across the cranking battery will be 12–13 volts depending on its state of charge; if it is below this then the battery is not well charged. When the engine is running, the alternator will put out enough electricity to raise this voltage to 14 volts once the battery is charged; if the battery is discharged it may take some time to reach this voltage. If the battery is deeply dis-

charged, 10 volts or less, the voltage should rise to 12–13 volts and remain at that level for several hours before rising to 14. At 14 volts the alternator decides that the battery is charged and reduces its current output to protect against over-charging.

The split charge relay is operated from the field coil of the alternator. When the engine is off, or the rpm is too low to run the alternator, the relay is off and there is no connection between the cranking battery positive and the service battery positive. As soon as the charging light on the alternator goes out when the engine comes up to speed, the relay activates and connects the two together; there will be a clear rise in the voltage across the service battery at this point. (See Chapter 3 for a more detailed look at the split charge relay.)

Batteries

The cranking battery has to put out a lot of power to turn over a diesel engine; these engines have a high compression ratio and can draw 100+ amps through the starter motor, so it is important to keep the cranking battery in good condition. Every month, and always before a cruise, inspect the electrolyte levels and top them up with distilled water if needs be; the level should be ¼in (6mm) above the top of the plates. A fully charged battery should read 13.2 volts on the volt meter at 10° C; however, it doesn't take long for a battery to lose this level of performance, and anything over 12.5 is acceptable. As the battery gets older it will become less efficient in cold weather, and after three or four years it may not cope with the demand placed on it by the starter motor. If it still holds a charge reasonably well it can probably do further work as a back-up battery for the cabin equipment.

The battery should have an insulating cover over it to prevent spanners dropping across the terminals. There should also be a good ventilator grille close by to allow the hydrogen and oxygen gases released during charging to vent overboard; these gases are explosive.

There are new varieties of battery now available, low maintenance types that don't need topping up, and gel types that have a semi-solid gel in place of the liquid electrolyte. The latter type are very good, but a narrow boat shouldn't need their anti-tilt benefits!

Wiring Loom

An engine has plenty of wires, all of which need to be checked for vibration damage. Copper is a wonderful conductor, but goes hard after repeated bendings and fractures. All the connectors to the temperature and pressure sensors need to be cleaned up, and a rub with a fine emery board will brighten the contacts. The high current wires to the starter motor and alternator need to have extremely clean connections and be bolted securely to their terminals. The ignition switch will need a squirt of aerosol lubricant into the keyhole if it is exposed to the elements. The battery isolator switch will also need an examination, and possibly a squirt of switch cleaner; this switch has to cope with the full starting current and needs to be up to the job, that is, with clean terminals securely tightened up.

Check the whole engine assembly for loose nuts and bolts, and the belts, pipes and wires for breaks before proceeding to the next stage.

Fuel and Filters

Oil Change

Once the engine is hot it can be turned off and

A sump pump is an invaluable aid to oil changing.

the hot oil pumped out. Older engines, especially those that were converted from van and lorry motors, may not have a sump pump fitted to them. It is possible to buy a little pump which will draw the old oil up through the dipstick hole; the alternative is to remove the drain-plug and let the oil drain into the oil drip tray, and then clean up the mess. In fact it makes *such* a mess that it is worth buying the pump just to avoid a couple of hours' cleaning!

The oil filter should be changed at the same time. These are usually spin-on type cartridges which in theory are done up hand-tight; however, getting them off is another matter. A chain wrench is the correct tool, which wraps around the filter and bites onto it as you unscrew it; they are a bit fiddly, but once you've got the knack they are marvellous. Stabbing a screwdriver through the filter and using this to unscrew it works just as well, although oil gets everywhere. When fitting the new filter, smear a little oil over the sealing washer to let it tighten up smoothly; put it on hand-tight, firm enough to make a good seal.

Old sump oil is not a pleasant substance: it contains all sorts of compounds, some of which are considered carcinogenic so it is a good idea to wear rubber gloves to keep the stuff off your hands, and to dispose of the oil at the local authority waste depot. If you suffer from dermatitis or eczema, treat it like a deadly poison.

Why bother with an oil change if the boat has only been used for a couple of hours since the last change a year ago? Oil degrades with time, condensation builds up in the sump, sediments accumulate, and lastly, diesel engines were built to run and if you don't run them, they will clog up. An oil change is essential to their ability to function. Anyway, if you are only running the engine for a couple of days a year then there is something fundamentally wrong, and you are not devoting enough time to boating.

Air filter on a Lister HB. Note the guard cage around the drive belt to prevent accidents.

Air Filters

Some engines have air filters, others not. If your motor has an air filter, check it and if necessary change it. Many motors simply have a screen on the air intake to keep the larger flies out; there isn't much left of the smaller ones by the time they have been subjected to the thousands of pounds per square inch in the cylinder. If your home mooring is a dusty place, for example near a foundry or a brickworks, then an air filter is a good idea since hard dust will score the piston and shorten the engine's life. Most boat engines are fitted in a comparatively dust-free compartment.

A frequently overlooked part of the air filter system is the crankcase breather tube.

On older engines this is usually just a small vent in the rocker cover; modern engines have a pipe from the rocker cover to the air filter. The vent allows the air in the crankcase to expand and contract as the pistons go up and down; it if becomes blocked the air pressure inside increases, forcing the oil out – it usually comes out of the dipstick hole. In this case the vent or tube should be checked to see that it is open.

After the oil change, restart the engine and run it for a few minutes; it should be much happier. Stop the engine for the next part of the service.

Fuel Filters

As mentioned earlier, where diesel fuel is concerned Cleanliness is very definitely next to Godliness. There should be at least one good quality fuel filter between the tank and lift pump, preferably with a separate water separator. This filter needs changing once a year, even if it doesn't appear to have become clogged up with dirt; but you don't want to wait until it is because as with most things, it will choose the most inconvenient time to let you down. With a new filter in place, at least this part of the fuel line will need to have the air bled out of it. There should be a bleed screw on the top of the filter, and the filter should be placed at a point where gravity will force the air out.

Purging the air from the fuel line is very important. How you actually do it varies according to installation but the principle is fairly constant. If gravity is not adequate to push the air out of the pipework, and it frequently isn't, decompress the cylinders, open the bleed valve just after the lift pump, and crank the engine over until the bubbles stop appearing from the bleed hole. Tighten down this valve and open the one between the injector pump and injectors, if there isn't one, then undo the injector pipe at the injector end. Crank the engine until fuel appears here. Retighten the pipe or bleed valve, and crank the engine over a few more times without compression. Close the decompressor and start her up – clouds of smoke and a hefty roar should result. The engine may hunt for a few minutes until the residual bubbles are all cleared, but after this it should run as sweet as anything.

The injector pipes take the pressurised fuel in metered doses to the injectors; they have

Fuel filter; note that the leak off-pipe returns to the tanks to reduce air locks.

Fuel shut-off tap.

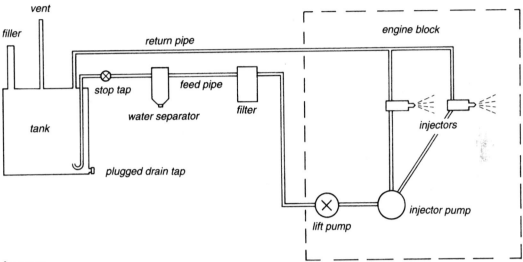

Fuel system.

to withstand massive pressures inside, and can leak very easily. Check that they are not rusting on the outside – even a small patch of rust can weaken the pipe enough to allow the fuel to burst out – and always treat them very carefully. The injectors themselves can only be cleaned and adjusted by a professional, so if the motor runs happily then leave them alone.

Bilge pump

No matter how well the self-draining decks work, a bilge pump is important. Holes in the hull of a boat are extremely rare, but if they do occur the bilge pump is going to be in demand. Check that it is in good working order. It may well be true that the best bilge pump in the world is a frightened man with a bucket, but it's best not to let it get that far!

Cleaning Out the Fuel Tank

The fuel tank on a narrow boat is usually a section of the stern swim, welded, closed and

fitted with filler and breather tubes, and the feed and return pipes to the engine. Current legislation is likely to change this arrangement so that boats will be fitted with removable tanks bolted into place. However, there will still be thousands of boats with the old design for decades to come, all facing the same inherent problem: apart from turning the boat upside-down and giving it a good shake, there is no way to get the accumulated dirt out of the tank. Some boats are fitted with a drain-plug which enables the tank to be cleaned easily, but not many.

The best way to clean out a tank with no drain-plug is to disconnect the fuel feed and return pipes. Fit a powerful pump on the feed pipe and suck the fuel out of the tank into a drum, through a fine filter. At the same time pump fresh fuel into the tank to stir up the sediments and water, rocking the boat as much as possible in the process. After a while this should stir up and remove most of the dirt. Reconnect the pipes, refill the tank and allow any remaining dirt to settle for twenty-four hours before bleeding the system.

Engine Replacement

A well installed and maintained engine will last ten or twenty years; a similar hull should last three times that at least, so a new engine is not uncommon for a boat. However, it is not simply a matter of shoe-horning in a new unit and pottering off up the cut: the engine, gearbox, reduction ratio and propeller are all part of a matched system and it is not possible to change one part without altering the performance of the others. The engine or gearbox are the most likely candidates for replacement. Gearboxes which contain the reduction ratio are made to a limited range of specifications, and so if your 2:1 ratio box expires, it is easy enough to get an exact replacement, and the system remains intact.

The same is unlikely to be true of the engine. They all generate rotational energy, but at different revolutions per minute in relation to their power. Older engines used to produce their full power at low revs, sometimes as low as 1,000 rpm. Modern engines, especially the ones derived from car engines, can run most effectively at 3,000, and sometimes more. This presents a problem when you want to replace an old unit that was putting out 10 horsepower at 1,000 rpm with a new engine with the same power output because it will probably only produce that power at 3,000 rpm. This means that you will need to get a new reduction gearbox, and since the old engine probably had a propeller designed to work off the old gearbox, the propeller may well need to be changed too,

Typical Cruiser-style layout.

since modern gearboxes may not have the correct reduction.

Fortunately engine manufacturers will provide a free design service so that you can get the most efficient transmission possible with their engine. There isn't a lot of point in trying to economize by keeping the old gearbox and sticking a new motor onto it; the chances are that it will be as worn out as the engine that you are having to replace, and will break down not long after.

A new engine is a very expensive part of the boat, and not only is it worth researching into who makes the engine most suited to your needs and budget, but also whether they will install it for you. There is a hidden benefit from this course of action, because not every engine that is sold is a perfectly running example of the engineer's craft. Some of them are out of specification, and sometimes they can be absolute rubbish. It isn't that common, but when a bad engine goes into a boat and fails to work, the repercussions are endless. The engineer who installs the engine tells the manufacturer that the engine is no good, then the manufacturer says that it was installed incorrectly. The engineer disagrees and points out faults, the manufacturer says the engine was all right on test. Meanwhile the poor boat owner has spent thousands of pounds and has a boat which needs to be towed by a horse to get anywhere – highly traditional, but not everyone's cup of tea.

It is important to ascertain before parting with money where the liabilities lie. A reputable engine manufacturer will have a network of trained fitters who will fit the engine, and then if anything is wrong with the motor there is a clear route to resolving the problem. It can cost more to deal with the companies which have trained agents, training courses for owners, and plenty of technical back-up, but in the long run the extra cost is worth it.

Towing a boat by hand is very hard work!

Hydraulic Drives

In recent years quite a few boats have been fitted with hydraulic drive systems. These provide much more versatility in layout, and the working principle is simple: the diesel engine drives an oil pump, and the oil is then piped to a motor which drives the propeller. The efficiency of modern drives is very good. Early systems tended to be made out of forklift truck components which were not designed for this type of application; they were forever breaking down and lost a lot of power. New systems are based on piston pumps and need little in the way of maintenance, and the hydraulic drive system has become popular because it allows the diesel engine to be placed virtually anywhere on the boat. In addition to this the motor can power a bow thruster and generator simultaneously.

The main driving thrust from the prop is taken directly to the hull at the hydraulic motor end of the system, allowing the engine to be mounted on softer, more sound-absorbent bearers.

Maintenance of the engine remains the same as an ordinary propulsion system. The hydraulic oil and its filters will need changing every so often, in accordance with the manufacturers' recommendation. These systems do tend to suffer from a few oil leaks whilst they are running in, but once bedded down they should provide years of trouble-free cruising.

Diesel Electric Drives

The basic physics of a diesel engine dictate that they are happiest working at their optimum revolutions per minute; at this speed they are at their most fuel-efficient, and last longest. One thing diesels detest is clanking along at barely more than tick-over speed: they soot up the cylinders and waste fuel. However, canal cruising rarely sees most engines having to do more than a tenth of their capacity; and let's face it, fully laden working boats plodded along at the speed limit with one horse or two donkeys as the maximum motive power. Modern narrow boats have 30 horsepower engines which can only be used at full throttle if they go between Sharpness and Bristol; anywhere else will cause bank erosion and destroy the canals that their owners profess to adore.

Diesel-electric systems are one way of using the engine to its optimum capability: the engine drives a generator, which in turn drives an electric motor turning the propeller; the system has been developed over the last decade and is beginning to show significant fuel savings. The latest generation of these drives uses a 3-phase electric generator and motor, providing a system as versatile as the hydraulic system. The diesel engine needs just as much maintaining, but the electrical side either works or not and shouldn't need maintenance at all.

Summary

The engine is the heart of the boat. No matter how pretty and luxurious the cabin is, the boat won't be going anywhere if the engine fails, unless it is downstream to the nearest weir. It provides the motive force of the boat, the electrical power, and not infrequently the heating as well. If you look after it, it should look after you. It is quite capable of giving decades of service as long as it is treated with respect, and given regular servicing and clean fuel which are its basic needs. However, engines are built to very fine tolerances whilst containing tremendous pressures: this means that they require specialist tools to carry out virtually any work other than basic servicing. So if you aren't qualified to work on them, please leave it to someone who is; and remember the adage: *If it ain't bust, don't fix it!*

3

The Electrical System

The electrical system on a narrow boat is almost invariably a 12-volt direct current one because the surplus power from the engine alternator is used to run the cabin equipment; the low voltage means that there is no risk of electrocution, making the system safer than the mains electricity at home. However, it is just as capable of starting a fire and must be treated carefully. A boat is a vehicle, and the electrical wiring is subjected to vibration, extremes of temperature and high humidity; for this reason it must be wired properly, using the correct wire, terminals and fuses.

As narrow boats have evolved into the sophisticated floating palaces we have now, the standards of wiring and equipment have improved, too. The old working boats had a radio and an accumulator cell as their complete electrical system, and some not even that. The first modern boats had very basic circuits, a few lights and pumps run off the engine's cranking battery, hooked together using any old wire. This wasn't at all satisfactory since the wire went hard from the vibration and broke, causing radio interference and equipment failure. The charge in the battery could also be used up on the lights, and the engine would then have to be hand-started.

Boat builders learnt a lot of tricks from caravan builders and now boats have two batteries, one solely for starting the engine and its equipment, and one for the cabin appliances. A device known as a split charge relay ensures that the two are only connected

Wire size guide for a 12-volt system					
Cross-sectional area of wire required in mm²					
Appliance type	Current demand	Distance from battery (m)			
(Typical)	(amps)	0–5	5–10	10–15	15–20
12 watt lamp	1	1	2	2	4
TV/stereo	3	2	2	4	4
Water pump	4	4	4	6	6
Fridge	6	4	6	6	8
Headlamp	8	6	6	8	8

together when the alternator is generating electricity. The result is that if a prolonged stop has meant the cabin battery is flat, the engine can still be started to generate more power.

The wiring has been upgraded to multi-strand automotive grade, and quite often the fuses have been replaced by miniature circuit breakers in domestic-style fuse boards. Boat builders have even realized that the special problem of low voltage systems is the resistance of the wire, and that the voltage drop caused by this resistance has to be taken into consideration when choosing the thickness of the wires.

New boats are being fitted with a tremendous range of equipment, the imagination and wealth of the owner being the only upper limit of what is possible. Washing machines, microwaves, and even word processors are finding their way onto narrow boats, all requiring a 240-volt alternating current

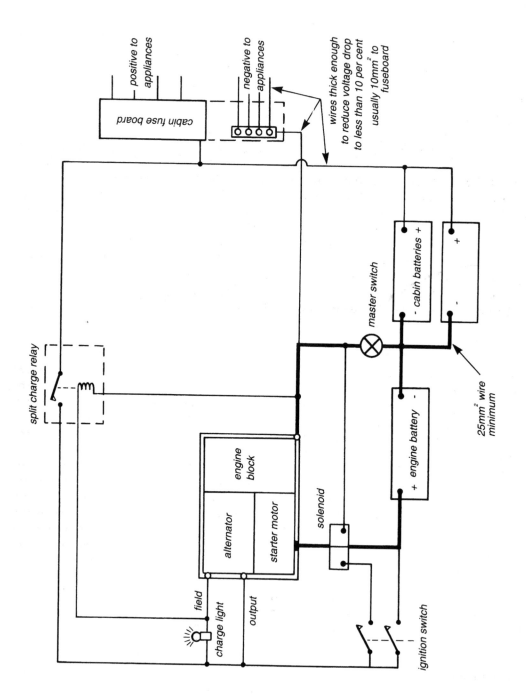

positive to appliances

cabin fuse board

negative to appliances

wires thick enough to reduce voltage drop to less than 10 per cent usually 10mm² to fuseboard

split charge relay

master switch

- cabin batteries +

+

-

25mm² wire minimum

engine block

+ engine battery -

alternator

starter motor

solenoid

field

charge light

output

ignition switch

Basic circuit diagram.

Clear signs and a neat layout are essential.

supply as we have in houses. These are driven by generators and inverters (considered separately at the end of this chapter).

The wiring system for a boat differs from a car in that the equipment has to have a wire from positive and a wire back to the negative of the battery, rather than having the negative grounded to the chassis or hull. This is because the negative would set up an electrochemical reaction between the hull and the water, leading to rapid corrosion of the steel. The system should be isolated from the hull, with the exception of the engine block, which is virtually impossible to isolate; and the radio aerial, which requires the hull to be earthed to receive the radio waves. This latter connection can be a cause of problems.

The Master Switch

A boat must have a battery master switch. This switch breaks the connection between the batteries and the circuits, both cabin and engine. It has to be able to pass the entire current when it is switched on, including the starter motor load, which means that it is a substantial switch, rated at 100–150 amps; also, the battery connectors must always be clean and firmly done up to allow this current to pass smoothly. The switch is normally between the batteries' negative and negative supply cables to both engine block and cabin circuit; this allows one switch to isolate both circuits. The heavy cable from the engine block to the battery must make very good contact at both ends.

At first glance this may not appear to be of life and death concern, but there is the matter of the radio aerial to be taken into account. If the negative from the engine block to the battery is poor, the electricity will find another route back to the battery, and the only one available is through the steel hull to the ground side of the radio aerial, down the aerial lead and back through the cabin wiring to

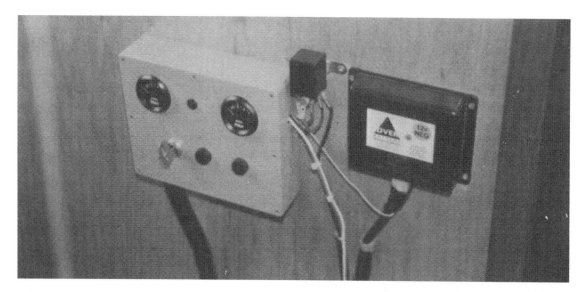

A battery management system.

the battery. The radio wiring circuit suddenly has to take 100+ amps when it is only built for a couple, and ignites as a result.

Clean contacts are very important all the time.

Charge Splitters

The alternator and batteries have been covered in Chapter 2. The split charge relay is not often prone to breakdown, and since it is a little black box there isn't much you can do except replace it if it breaks. It is possible to use a diode charge splitter instead of a relay, a solid state electronic component which only allows electricity to pass in one direction. However, there is a slight voltage drop across the component which reduces the total charge of the cabin battery. New versions of this electronic device are being developed to improve its performance. It is also possible to get 'battery management controllers' which make the alternator charge up the batteries to their full capacity.

All these electronic controllers work on

The ultimate split charge system, two *alternators!*

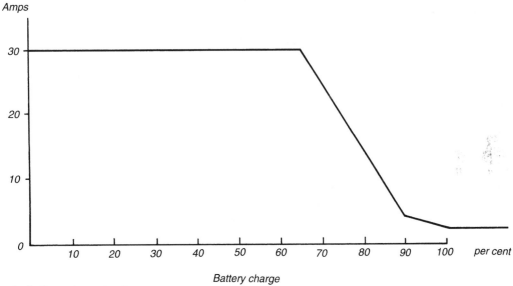

Typical alternator output.

the premise that the engine alternator will shut down its output when it senses 14 volts on the output wire to the battery (voltage sensing alternators are the automotive industry standard). However, you can get 'battery sensing' alternators that have a separate wire to the battery and keep the charge going until the battery is properly charged. They cost quite a lot more. The electronic controllers aren't cheap, either, and all of them are well in excess of the price of a second or third battery. If you are having to worry about the battery not holding enough power, a second battery will double the power available, and should solve the problem. Moreover the controllers and diodes are little black boxes too, and therefore unserviceable, so breakdown requires replacement.

The electrical system on a boat needs to be able to work without breakdowns since these can be a serious fire hazard. The design principle 'Keep It Simple' should be the rule, although some new boats seem to have forgotten this.

Inspection and Maintenance of the Wiring

The wires conducting the power to the lights and pumps should be accessible. Short runs behind the cabin lining are acceptable, but the majority of the wires should be in a duct where they can be examined at least once a year. If the wires are a good automotive grade they shouldn't be in any danger of breaking up, but it does no harm to check. The insulation should be the colour it was when installed, and the wire should remain pliable; if the insulation is starting to look discoloured and the wire is going hard, there is a strong possibility that the wire is getting hot under load, caused by it carrying more current than it is supposed to. The final outcome of this situation if it is left unchecked is that the wire can cause a fire.

Overloading

When a wire becomes suspect like this the

first thing to do is to check how much power is going through it. Boats accumulate equipment as they get older, and a cable that was originally installed to run one fluorescent light drawing one amp, can end up having to supply the current for three lights and a television whose total current load will be about five amps; and if the wire originally installed was only suitable for one amp, it will get rather hot with five. The equipment run off it will work badly as well, because as the maximum current loading of a wire is approached, the resistance of the wire plays an important role in reducing the voltage at the end; the longer the cable, the greater this voltage drop will be.

This overloading of cables is a common problem. The solution is either to wire each appliance directly to the fuse board with the proper cable, or to replace the wire with a suitable grade and add another fuse board closer to where the various appliances are connected to it. The former method is by far the simplest in the long run.

Wire Mounting

The wires need to be clipped securely so that they do not rattle about and chaff. They also need to be laid out neatly so that each one can be clearly identified; there have been plenty of accidents caused by confusion as to which wire goes where. Ducting is the best solution to keeping this potential spaghetti under control; the duct can be fixed to the roof and covered with an ornamental wooden fascia.

Fuses

The fuse board on a boat is the heart of the electrical wiring. Each appliance needs to have its own fuse which will be rated to blow at a current slightly more than the unit will demand, and less then the maximum current capacity of the wire. This way, if the appliance short-circuits, the fuse will blow before the wire sets on fire. Fuse boards come in a variety of types: the straightforward automotive ones are very suitable for small and

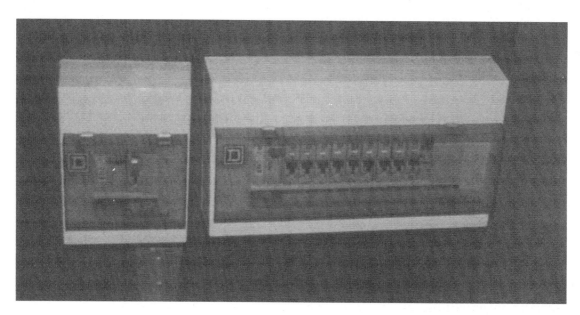

The boat's fuse board, with a separate board for the 240-volt circuit.

uncomplicated boats, and the large domestic consumer units are often used for boats with a huge array of equipment; these can be fitted with miniature circuit breakers of the appropriate current rating. There are specialist marine fuse boards which are already clearly marked for navigation lights, bilge pumps and so on, and which combine utility with a smart, efficient presentation.

Problems of Older Boats

What *should* be in a boat is not always the same as what *is* in there, especially on older boats. If the wiring on your boat resembles something left by a drunken spider rather than a neat and tidy piece of electrical engineering, it may be a good idea to rip it all out and replace it. Old systems rarely take any account of the voltage drop along a wire's length, so that your television at the bows may only be getting 10 volts even though the battery at the stern is at 12. The current capacity of the wire may not be anything like what is required for, say, the water pump, and quite a lot of the cables may be placed behind the cladding in contact with polystyrene insulation, which can destroy PVC electrical insulation.

Rewiring

A fresh start is the best solution to an ageing wiring system. We think nothing of a house needing to be rewired, and the same is true of a boat. The apparent upheavel need not be too great because the latest regulations suggest that all cables should be mounted in a position where they can be inspected, which means ducts; these can usually be installed in the corner of the cabin ceiling. The work is quite simple if you are good at DIY and understand the principles behind low voltage wiring. If you are not, don't tackle it yourself – a burnt-out boat can be the result of an error in the circuit.

New boats are wired in accordance with the BMEA (British Marine Electricians Association) Code of Practice, and if you are rewiring an old boat it is worth making sure that the new wiring meets these guidelines. They are not particularly onerous, although the formulae for working out the cable sizes needed for a given load over a specific distance might make your hair curl.

Inspection and Maintenance of Appliances

A small narrow boat will probably have only half-a-dozen lights, a pair of water pumps, a

Boats are fitted with plenty of electrical appliances these days.

radio/cassette player and a socket for a television. Larger boats can come with all sorts of other appliances including cooker hoods, electric food blenders and stereo systems: all of these need some looking after.

Lights

The simple filament light bulb requires nothing more than the bulb changing when it blows. The switch may become corroded by damp air after a few years and need replacing, but this is unlikely if a good quality switch is used. Halogen light bulbs have a powerful light output, although some varieties also emit the ultraviolet light that is alleged to cause skin cancer, and are therefore a theoretical risk.

Fluorescent lights can be more demanding. They are popular because they provide a lot more light than a filament bulb of the same power, but there is more that can go wrong with them. A 12-volt fluorescent unit comprises a switch, a small inverter to boost the voltage high enough to run the tube, and the tube itself. Most of the sort fitted in boats are built for the caravan market, but because caravans are not as humid as boats the switches are usually prone to corrosion; this reduces the power available to the inverter and results in a flickering light, or apparent failure. The units are cheap enough to replace, rather than repair, although if they have been designed so that you can get at the switch (which a few are) a clean-up of the contacts can restore them.

A remote-controlled searchlight is ideal for tunnels.

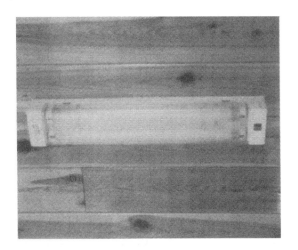

Fluorescent tubes often need a radio interference suppressor fitted.

The tubes last a long time, and when the ends start to become discoloured and the brightness fades, new ones can be obtained from a chandlery or caravan shop.

The real problem with some fluorescent lights is the radio interference that the inverter generates; it emits a high-pitched whine into the electrical wiring and can interfere with radio and television reception. An interference suppressor – available from car accessory shops – can be fitted close to the unit to reduce this.

Several lights can be run from one fuse as long as the fuse rating is below that of the wire.

Radio, TV and Cassette Players

Radios have problems picking up signals inside a boat, and need an external aerial on the roof. Low bridges rip these straight off, so a telescopic one is a good compromise as long as you keep the segments well greased; they will seize up and snap if allowed to get dry. Fibreglass whip aerials are much sturdier, as long as they can fold down flat on the roof whilst you are cruising.

Cassette players provide pleasant music, but a boat is a humid environment which plays havoc with the tapes and tape-head. Most cassette players will need to have a tape-head cleaner played through them once a month if they are to perform at optimum quality.

Televisions seem to be able to stand the damp, but can be difficult to tune in; like a radio, they have trouble getting a clear signal inside a steel shell. An external aerial is the best solution, and even then a signal booster amplifier can often be the only way to get a good picture. A major part of the reception difficulties derives from the fact that many canals, and all rivers, are at the bottom of valleys where there is a poor line of sight to the television transmitter. Dancing around the boat with the aerial held over your head may keep your crew amused, but it rarely results in a better picture. A good book may be a simpler solution for an evening's entertainment!

All these three need to have an interference suppressor fitted as well as their own fuse. The handbook for each one will state the fuse size.

Water Pumps

The boat will have one pump to pressurize the plumbing system, and one to pump out the shower tray. For the plumbing part, see Chapter 4; the electrical connections are the same as for any appliance, that is, take the positive and negative wires back to the fuse board and make sure the fuse rating is correct. The terminals on the pumps are subject to more vibration than the other equipment, so need an extra check to make sure they are not working loose.

The bilge pump can be fitted with an automatic switch to ensure that it will turn on if the bilges fill with rainwater. Since it is good practice to turn off the boat's electrical system when it is unattended, this switch will need to be wired directly to the battery, bypassing the master switch. It *must* have its own fuse. The switches are usually floats that operate the electrical switch, and reputable manufacturers make these very rugged and weatherproof so they will need no maintenance – cheap switches for this application are a waste of time.

Burglar Alarms

As the value of the equipment on a boat rises, so does the temptation for thieves to have a go at removing it. An alarm system for a boat is subtly different to that of a car, although the basic circuit is similar. Most car alarms trigger if the vehicle moves, which would be a complete disaster on a bobbing boat. The intruder sensors of a boat alarm need to be either pressure mats set under the carpets along the corridor, or passive infra-red proximity detectors; both these types of sensor will be unaffected by the boat's movement. Of the two, the pressure mats consume no power until triggered, whereas the infra-red detectors will use a small amount constantly. The sensors will need to trigger a siren loud enough to attract the attention of the boatyard staff, or whoever is closest – in rural districts this may mean a *very* loud siren. However, the law states that it shouldn't be so loud as to cause permanent damage to a burglar's hearing. Like bilge pumps, burglar alarms will need to be connected directly to the battery, bypassing the master switch; they too must have the correct fuse fitted to them.

Gas Detectors

A gas detector is the only other piece of equipment that should be connected directly to the battery with its own fuse. The latest generation of gas detectors consumes significantly less power than the early designs, although they do still represent a considerable drain on the battery when left working continuously for months on end. Like so many pieces of electronic equipment, there is no maintenance involved apart from testing every few months that they work. If they fail they cannot be repaired unless you are specifically qualified to do so.

Cooker Extractor Fans

A cooker hood has a filter built into it which catches the grease and steam, but this can become a source of rancid smells if it isn't renewed periodically. The flue from the hood to the outside can also get clogged up after many years of use, and now and again will need a clean with a strong degreaser. Most cooker hoods are built with a fluorescent light in them, though quite why remains a mystery since the tube always seems to be coated with grease and fails to illuminate the cooker. It is important to remember that the electronic inverter in these units may only be a tiny little thing, but it can still give you a jolt if you touch the terminals with wet fingers. The light must be switched off before you remove the tube for cleaning, and the tube must be completely dry before being replaced.

Bilge Blowers

Bilge blowers are not a common appliance on narrow boats but they serve a useful function, clearing out stale moist air and any residues of gas that lurk at the bottom of the boat. Electrically they are simple and trouble-free.

Most other low-voltage accessories are plug-in ones. Every socket in the boat must be wired with the grade of wire and fuse that will support the largest of them. A 10-amp load is the largest load that a portable appliance is likely to need.

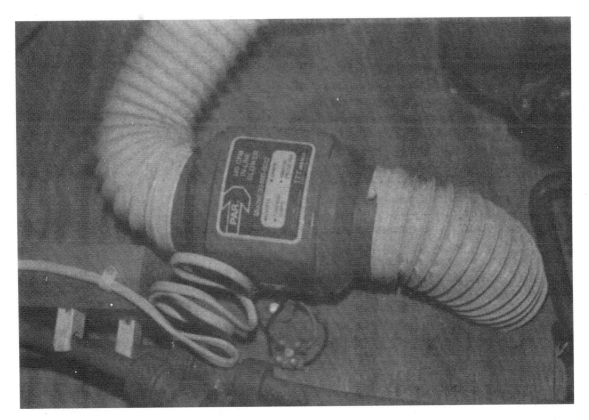

A bilge blower.

Generators

Larger boats tend to be used for more extended cruising, and allow more room for some of life's little luxuries. As a result, owners of full-sized boats are installing mains-powered equipment such as washing machines, microwaves, even electric blankets. Heaven knows what the boatman of yesteryear would have thought of it all; the electric blankets would have been very popular, I suspect! These items can only be powered by normal mains power, which can be supplied to a boat via a shore line plugged into a socket ashore, a generator, or an inverter which converts stored power in the batteries to mains type power.

Mistakes with mains power can be very serious. A frayed wire can mean instant death, and so it is crucially important that any mains installation is tested by an electrician at least every twelve months, and more often than that if the system is being used on a full-time basis. The shore lines are very susceptible to damage. There are plenty of safety regulations for your system to meet, and it is your responsibility to make sure that your boat is safe. There are no mandatory safety rules about 240-volt installations aboard boats, but the British Marine Electronics Association has covered the area thoroughly in its Code of Practice; the guidance in this will enable a system to be installed which will meet all future safety legislation as well as being safe to use.

Generators systems aboard narrow boats

A built-in 240-volt generator.

fall into two categories, portable and fixed. The portable, often petrol-fuelled generator provides a reasonable amount of power in a convenient package, and for loads up to a kilowatt it is perfect, except for one big drawback: petrol is a volatile, dangerous fuel. It is rarely used for narrow boat engines for this very reason, and there isn't much point in spending thousands of pounds to have a safe diesel engine to push the boat along, and then carry petrol cans on board for the generator. If you do, the generator and petrol must be stored on the boat where it will be safe. The type of locker used for storing bottle gas is generally in a good position because any petrol vapour will vent overboard, though unfortunately most boats only have one gas locker, usually already filled with gas bottles. It isn't very secure to keep the generator and fuels cans on the deck, but it is the only other safe place for them; the generator can probably be chained and padlocked to the hull.

Under no circumstances should the generator and fuel cans be brought into the cabin because the chance of the cooker or fire igniting the petrol vapour is far too high.

Maintenance of small petrol engines is much the same as for any motor; follow the manufacturers' instructions and don't do more than they suggest. It can be difficult to assess how many hours a small unit has run for, and they are fussy about having regular oil changes; however, it is possible to get an electronic hour gauge which will remind you when an oil change is due.

A more permanent power generation system can be obtained by fitting a small diesel generator; it will be able to run off the boat's fuel tank at a much lower cost than a petrol unit. The manufacturers are making some very sophisticated generators nowadays, which make virtually no noise, switch themselves on when you want them to, and provide a clean, stable power supply; their maintenance needs are low, too. Built-in diesel generators have to be cooled, and a keel cooling tank is not sufficient for this. Normal installation practice is to have them cooled by water from the canal with a wet exhaust, which is quiet and effective but suffers from all the problems associated with the system. The maintenance of the engine is virtually identical to that of the main engine.

Modern generators are usually housed in a soundproof enclosure, making them far less intrusive than the little petrol things. You would hardly know they were there, and in fact most people seem to forget them altogether until they go wrong. To avoid any sudden breakdowns, do follow all the advice laid down in the manufacturers' literature.

Inverters

Inverters are a secondary source of 240-volt power for intermittent use, but unless you are prepared to spend a lot of money on a really good system, they will not match the stability or cleanliness of electricity supplied by a generator. The devices take power stored in a large battery bank and convert it from 12 volts DC to 240 AC. They are useful for appliances like hoovers and food processors, not so good for microwaves, and virtually hopeless for fridges. As with generators, they need to be fitted by qualified fitters if the boat is going to have a permanent 240-volt ring main.

An inverter requires a large battery bank: 400 amp hours is suitable for an 800-watt unit, and this has to be charged from the engine's alternator. For larger systems a high output alternator will need to be fitted instead of the normal 30-amp type. This will place an additional load on the fan belt, which you will need to inspect more

An inverter battery bank. It is always best to renew all the batteries in the bank at the same time.

An inverter and charger.

often. The charge/discharge cycle of the battery bank will be much greater than that of an ordinary boat, and the volume of hydrogen and oxygen gas given off will be proportionally greater. The installation and maintenance of the batteries is therefore that much more critical.

There must be at least thirty square inches of ventilator grill in the battery compartment, and all the switches and equipment in this area should be ignition protected so that no stray sparks can ignite any lingering gases. Ideally the batteries should have a compartment to themselves that is only ventilated overboard, although they will need to be easily accessible as the electrolyte levels will need checking once a week when the inverter is in regular use. Once a year each battery will

need to be individually tested to check it is still working correctly. They should have a life expectancy of three to five years. It is normal practice to use 'deep cycle' batteries for this application as they have a higher antimony content in the plates to make them harder, and they can cope with a full charge/discharge cycle better than an ordinary engine cranking battery. They cost considerably more, of course. Good quality cranking batteries will work fairly well, but have a slightly shorter life-span.

The electricity produced by the generator is the same as the stuff that comes from the power stations: a sine wave oscillating at fifty cycles per second. The on-board generator might not be quite as stable as a nuclear power station, but it isn't far off it. Some

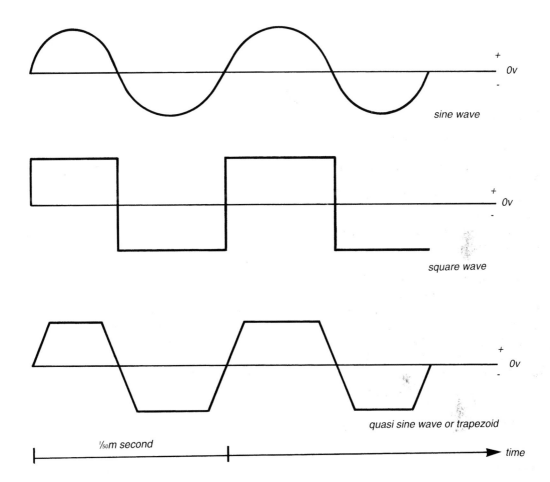

sine wave

square wave

quasi sine wave or trapezoid

¹/₅₀m second

time

Inverter wave forms.

inverters can produce this type of power but they are very expensive; most produce a rather rougher version called clipped square wave, trapezeoid, or quasi sine wave, a filtered square wave which will transmit the power to most appliances, but which can leave some electric motors and electronic equipment juddering.

There are only a few companies who will advise and install inverters; there are plenty who will sell a dubious unit to the unsuspecting. If you intend to install one yourself, and are qualified to do so, the major points to bear in mind are: battery bank capacity, battery ventilation, engine alternator capacity, and wiring safety.

Mains-powered Equipment

Once a boat is equipped to power mains equipment, the sky is more or less the limit, space allowing. Some commonly fitted appliances are these:

Dishwashers: Most boaters would consider these to be decadent, but apparently they consume less water per load than their human equivalent, and they don't complain that the tea towel has gone soggy.

Washing machines: These consume vast amounts of water, but as anyone with a small child will confirm, they are essential. Launderettes used to be the mainstay of cruising clothes cleaning, but they are disappearing from the canal-side villages, along with all the other shops.

Microwaves: Easy and fast way of heating food. They aren't everyone's idea of cooking, but they are popular nevertheless.

Hoovers: Anyone who has ever tried to clean the carpet of a full-length narrow boat with one of those pathetic little car cleaners will appreciate a proper hoover.

Word processors: Essential bit of kit! Like hair-driers.

Fridges, heaters and clocks are not really suitable for this power source because of their continuous power demand; you wouldn't be popular with other boaters if your generator, no matter how quiet, kept turning itself on and off all through the night.

All equipment needs to be looked after just as well as it is at home.

Summary

The wiring on a boat is a system which can provide the boater with plenty of home comforts, but it needs to be carefully designed to work continuously, without breakdowns. Faults in the system can constitute a major fire risk, and so regular inspection is essential. Alterations to the system need to be planned and evaluated so that they don't overload the existing circuit. Any work required on the circuit needs to be carried out to professional standards of workmanship.

As the design of boats has improved, the demands boaters put on the electrical system

The more equipment you have, the bigger the fuse board needs to be.

have increased. The complexity of a modern boat, complete with 240-volt power system, is almost certainly beyond the experience of the well-intentioned amateur, and it needs a properly qualified electrical engineer to inspect it for faults.

— 4 —

The Plumbing System

The plumbing system on a narrow boat is very similar to that in a house, and if the boat has been well made it will require only a minimum of attention throughout the life of the boat. Its special feature is that it is self-contained, having a large tank for clean water and another to hold foul water with the appropriate pumps to ensure adequate water pressure and drainage.

Water systems have changed little over the thirty years of modern narrow boat construction, apart from the introduction of frostproof pipes and the more widespread use of waste-holding tanks. There is a tendency to install plastic or stainless steel tanks in new boats, rather than have built-in ones and these are more hygienic and easier to keep clean.

The system consists of a tank, coarse filter, pressurizing pump, pipework, taps, shower drain pump, drain outlets through the hull, toilet, holding tank and occasionally an evacuation pump.

The water-tank filler needs to be clearly marked. This boat also has a bug-proof tank ventilator.

Tanks

The most basic and common water tank is a welded compartment beneath the foredeck; it can hold a very large volume of water, often in excess of two hundred gallons. The design is cheap to construct but has several inherent drawbacks, and as with most system designs, the drawbacks usually mean more maintenance. The tank should have an inspection cover set in the top and a filler pipe with a clearly labelled screw cover. However, this type of inspection cover has the snag that if it

is not a watertight fit it will allow muddy rainwater to leak from the deck into the tank. The gasket or sealant needs to be in good condition and the bolts done up firmly. Every year, and at the most every two, the cover will need to be removed and the tank cleaned out and painted with water tank paint; if you keep on top of this cleaning schedule it needn't be an onerous task. Although the water that appears out of a tap may look sparklingly clean, it will actually contain a fair amount of the sand and debris which always settles to the bottom of a tank; if you leave the boat for a decade without cleaning it, the extra work might put you off boating for life particularly as the sediment can become quite offensive.

The inside walls of the tank must be inspected for rust and cracks. A small pin-hole crack will allow the canal water to mix with your drinking water, even though the boat's buoyancy will not be affected, and canal water is not good for your health. When the tank is cleaned out and scrubbed, a fresh coat of tank black (a type of bituminous paint designed for this task) can be applied. If possible the lid should be left off for a few days to allow all the solvents to evaporate before sealing the tank down.

Plastic and stainless steel tanks do not suffer from the same corrosion problems and can be left longer before being cleaned out. Since they are usually quite light, it is quite possible to unbolt them and take them off the boat for a good hose out. Cleaning them in situ is also quite feasible, in which case empty the tank, and add a few gallons of sterilizing solution – the products suitable for babies' bottles are ideal. Shake the tank vigorously, or rock the boat to stir up the sediments, and pump the tank out; then flush through with plenty of clean water, and that should be all that is needed.

Tank cleanliness is important: quite a number of bacteria thrive in dark stagnant water and can cause serious stomach upsets, and no one wants to have this happen whilst on holiday. The old-fashioned built-in tanks are all too prone to this sort of problem.

A further drawback of the built-in tank is the effect that it can have on the boat's stability when it is half full. A hundred gallons of water sloshing to one side of the boat can make a small list into a big one, and when this 500 kilogram wave rebounds back to the other side of the tank, the boat starts to lurch all over the place. It is not impossible to fit baffles into an existing tank to slow the water

down and thus reduce the wash, but it is difficult.

Sometimes a built-in tank is simply the front two feet of the bows, the triangular tank being formed by the two sides curving into the stem post and a vertical bulkhead, and the hatch used to cover the hay locker being both filler and inspection. This design has to be the very worst for stability since the centre of gravity of the water is so high; and the design doesn't rate very highly for cleanliness either, since every insect and bug that feels like it can just jump in.

If you have had a look inside your built-in tank and don't like what you see, all is not lost. There are several companies which custom-make a butyl rubber liner that can be inserted into the old tank space, thus providing a new tank inside the old one.

Filters

There should be a filter between the tank and the water pump to catch all the flecks of rust and sand grains which would otherwise block up or wear out the pump. Modern pumps are usually made of plastic, and the moving parts wear away surprisingly quickly if they have to pump abrasive particles. The usual filter is a fine wire screen which can be removed from the filter housing and given a good scrub and rinse to remove the debris – though before dismantling it, don't forget to close the tank's stop cock!

There is also a range of charcoal filters available which do much more than simply catch the sediments: they react with any chemical contamination, binding it into the filter structure. They are very effective and can be fitted into the pipework quite easily, and their maintenance is simply a matter of replacing them when they have filtered out so much rubbish that the water can no longer flow through them easily. They are normally fitted either in the main pipe from the pump

Charcoal water filter.

switch mounted in each tap, so when the tap is turned on, a contact is made and the pump runs. This is fine for a small Cruiser, but the wire runs on a narrow boat are so long that the voltage drop through them is likely to reduce the effectiveness of the pump; also the maintenance of this system can be tricky. The switch contacts in the taps are very prone to corrosion because of the proximity to water, but they are not easy to reach for cleaning. If you have this system, it is also worth putting a voltmeter across the pump terminals whilst it is running to check whether the long runs of wire have reduced the voltage too much.

Most boats have the pressurized pump system. This has a pressure-operated switch which turns the pump on when the water pressure in the pipe drops below a certain point. Assuming that there aren't any leaks in the pipework, this happens when a tap is opened. The switch keeps the pump running until the pressure is regained, which can only happen after the tap is closed again. The usual range of switching pressures are around one bar to start the pump, and two bar to stop it.

Pressure Switches

The pressure switch is often mounted within the pump and can either be a solid state electronic device or an interesting arrangement of diaphragms, springs and adjusting screws. The solid state switches are a lot less trouble to set up. Mechanical switches are normally preset to cut in and out at the right pressure, and unless there is a very good reason to alter them, don't bother.

Pressure switches are prone to 'pipe hammer'. This is when a shock wave is caused by the pump turning off quickly: it travels along the pipe, bounces back, re-triggers the pressure switch creating another shock wave, and so on. The result is that the pump doesn't shut off cleanly, but buzzes to halt. In a domestic house this pipe hammer

outlet, thus purifying the entire water system, or just in the pipe to the kitchen cold tap that supplies drinking water; the latter case means that the filter will have to clean less water, and so will last longer. Most charcoal filters contain a silver additive to prevent bacterial growth in the water when it is left standing for prolonged periods.

Pumps

The pressurizing pump is quite capable of ruining your holiday by breaking down at an inconvenient moment. You just can't get the water out of the tank without it, so it is worth looking after. Pumping systems fall into two categories: those that maintain a constant pressure in the pipes at all times, and those that are switched on by electric switches mounted in the taps. Virtually all new narrow boats are fitted with the first type.

The switched pump systems have a small

Mechanical pressure switch.

can be a real nuisance, rattling all the pipes; on a boat it isn't so loud, but the contacts of the pressure switch can become pitted by the arcing that the process causes.

Accumulator Tanks

A good way to ensure a smooth water flow is to fit an accumulator tank to a pressurized system. This is a tank containing a few litres of air. The pump compresses the air as well as the water in the pipes, forcing a litre or so of water into the bottom of the tank; this forms a reservoir so that if you only draw off a cupful the pump needn't turn on. The air also acts as a cushion for any shock waves caused by the pump, making the system quieter. It shouldn't require any maintenance.

Pump Maintenance

Most water pumps for boats are self-priming types, though they don't often need to be, since the pump is usually located at the lowest point in the water system. They are usually 'diaphragm' types and comparatively long-lived, though the manufacturers supply repair kits consisting of a new diaphragm and any valve flaps and gaskets that the pump may need. It is worth keeping a repair kit on the boat.

The maintenance of the pump is mostly a matter of keeping the water it pumps clean. It is counter-productive to dismantle the thing to see if it is all right, as the sealing gaskets will probably break as you do it. Some of the cheaper makes of pump cannot be dismantled or repaired, and in this case it is worth keeping a spare pump on board. However, two cheap pumps are more expensive than one good one, so a cheap pump is a false economy.

When fitting a new pump it can help to prime it up by putting a cup of warm water containing a few drops of olive oil through it; this lubricates the valves. The water pump is the most likely piece of electrical equipment to suffer from voltage drop, as it is almost invariably at the opposite end of the boat to the batteries. On a full-size boat this means that the power has to travel a round trip of a hundred and forty feet (43m). The resistance of the wire over this distance becomes an important factor, and it is a good idea to check the voltage across the pump's terminals to ensure that it is getting the correct voltage. It may be that a heavier gauge wire needs to be fitted.

Pipework

The nature of boats as holiday craft means that they are usually laid up over the winter;

the interior then cools off to the temperature of the outside air, and naturally they freeze up. This can cause a lot of damage to a water system that hasn't been either designed or prepared for it.

Pipe Layout and Draining

A narrow boat plumbing system is best drained down if the boat is not going to be used over the winter, and to facilitate this the pipes need to be installed so that all the water in them can run down to a lowest point, and the drain tap located there. Most people visit their boat every week regardless of the weather, and it is possible to divide the hot and the cold parts of the system, and drain down only the hot side; water heaters, especially the gas ones, are very vulnerable to frost damage. Besides, protecting the plumbing against freezing yet still being able to make a cup of tea on board appeals to most boaters.

Pipe Materials

Copper pipes are likely to split if the water in

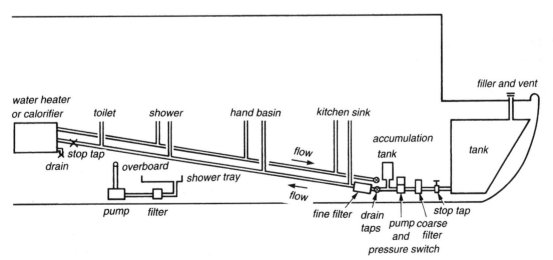

Basic plumbing system with appropriate falls for drain down.

Pipework with drain-cock.

them freezes, and it is a matter of urgency to drain the water out before the first frosts. Draining them down must be completed properly, too, because even just a little water left lying in a dip in the pipe can burst the copper. (The alternative to draining down is to add an antifreeze to the system, see p.79.)

Repairing a fractured copper pipe involves cutting out the affected length and replacing it, and this is not an easy task since the pipes are often at the back of cupboards or lockers. Moreover the pipe will be distorted by the ice for some distance either side of the break in it, and you may need to replace a metre of pipe for a half-inch-long hole. Repairs are best carried out with compression fittings because soldering pipes close to that amount of wood without setting it ablaze is a very skilled task.

Plastic 'frostproof' pipe is used extensively in boat plumbing nowadays, and it has many advantages over traditional copper pipe: the plastic is able to expand to accommodate

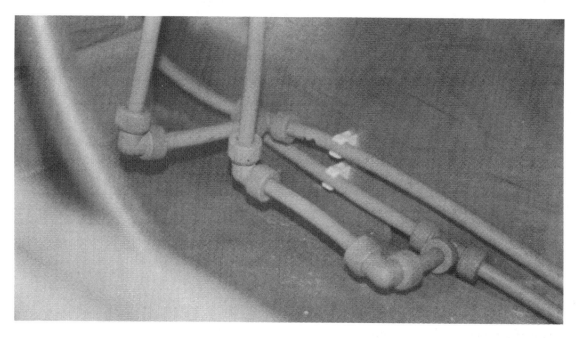

Pipework showing poorly assembled joints which may blow apart in frost.

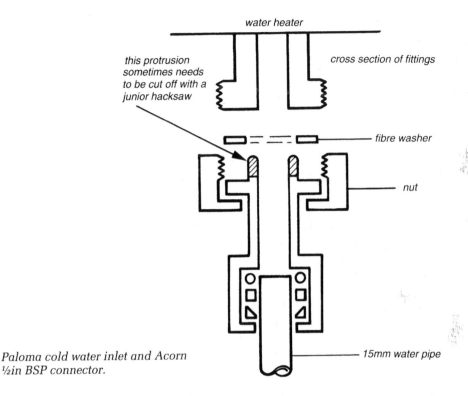

water heater

this protrusion
sometimes needs
to be cut off with a
junior hacksaw

cross section of fittings

fibre washer

nut

15mm water pipe

*Paloma cold water inlet and Acorn
½in BSP connector.*

the greater volume that the ice demands; it is available with push-on connectors that make construction of the system very quick and easy; and its flexibility helps in routeing it around the various curves of the boat. It is slightly more expensive than copper, but when the benefits of the material are taken into account, the argument for it becomes compelling. However, it is not suitable for the very high temperatures that some solid fuel stoves can generate.

Plastic pipe comes with a complete range of fittings to enable easy installation. The only catch is that the ½in BSP connector has a protruding edge which normally fits inside the ½in male thread it connects to, and on some appliances this protrusion prevents the washer and flange making a firm contact with

the pipe. The protrusion needs to be sawn off flush with a junior hacksaw.

The beauty of this pipework is that connections are made simply by pushing the pipe (with its internal support sleeve) into the fitting; a smear of silicon lubricant can ease this, and the pipe marked with arrows so you can see that it has been fully pushed home. Taking it apart, however, is well nigh impossible, so it is important to plan the work in advance. Plastic pipework is compatible with copper, thus a frost-damaged section of copper can be replaced with frostproof plastic pipe.

Pipe Sizes

The water flow generated by most pressure

A calorifier.

pumps is in the region of ten litres (two gallons) a minute. This is more than adequate for a narrow boat, unless it is a large boat where more than one shower will be operating simultaneously. Ordinary 15mm-diameter pipe will be fine for the water supply, with 12mm (½in) taps. On small boats where only a small shower and sink need to be supplied, clear plastic 10mm pipe can be used. Central heating systems require larger pipe sizes if they are to be run using gravity (see Chapter 5).

Water Heaters

Most boats use either a gas instantaneous water heater or a calorifier heated by the engine. For the last few years there has increasingly been a move away from gas-fired appliances on boats for safety reasons, and the calorifier provides a low-cost alternative to gas-fired heating systems.

Plumbing in a calorifier is simplicity itself: there is a feed and return from the engine's cooling circuit, and a feed from the cold water and outlet for the hot. The units can be crammed into all sorts of corners to keep them out of the way, and once fitted should require no maintenance.

Gas heaters must now be serviced once a year by a CORGI (Council of Registered Gas Installers) Engineer, and the regulations concerning gas heaters are increasingly stringent because they have been the cause of several fatalities. If the flue becomes blocked, the incomplete combustion of the gas generates carbon monoxide: this then quietly and insidiously suffocates the occupants of the boat, and there is little or no warning that they are in danger.

Water heaters are also fitted with a short-ened flue. This can cause the pilot light to be blown out, or a strong wind can blow the exhaust gases back down into the boat, both of which circumstances can cause serious problems. It is therefore one of the most important aspects of boat maintenance that these gas-fired heaters be properly serviced, by qualified engineers. (See Chapter 5 for more detail.)

Antifreeze

The best way to avoid frost damage is to remove the water, but this is not always pos-sible and then it is essential to use an antifreeze solution; water heaters in particu-lar, whether gas, solid fuel or calorifiers, can be extremely expensive to replace. Unlike the cooling system for an engine, the water system inside a boat is required to supply drinking water, and ordinary automobile antifreeze contains ethylene glycol which is toxic. A different, potable, product therefore has to be used, which consists of a non-toxic sugar solution. To charge the pipes with it, empty the system, pour a couple of gallons into the tank, and let the pump push it through all the pipes; it is important to ensure that it has penetrated the entire system. In the spring the solution is then flushed out with plenty of fresh water.

On the whole, this is an expensive alterna-tive to simply draining the system down, and an object lesson in the value of designing the plumbing so that it can be maintained properly.

Drainage

The disposal of waste water is simple enough: it goes over the side. The soap helps break up the diesel spilt into the water, and the scraps of food feed the fish. The kitchen sink and bathroom basin drain directly through a skin-fitting in the hull; usually the pipe from the plug-hole to the skin-fitting is a plastic one held in place by a pair of jubilee clips, and it is important to check these clips at least annually to make sure they are not rusting away.

If the hull skin-fitting is within eight inches (20cm) of the water-line it should have two clips securing the flexible section to the steelwork. Stainless steel jubilee clips can be fitted to avoid the corrosion problem. The pipe must be brought up above eight inches of the water-line before reaching the sink outlet.

Shower Drain Pumps

The shower cannot drain by gravity since the plug-hole is below the water-line, so it has to be pumped overboard, and there have been a variety of ingenious ways to deal with this. On some of the first boats the water was allowed to run into the bilges, and was then pumped out with the existing bilge pump. This is not a sensible idea. Ordinary water pumps have been used but with varying degrees of success, further exacerbated by the fact that very few boat builders fit filters in front of the shower drain pump. The shower water contains human hair which is tough stuff and can tangle up a small impeller-type pump with monotonous regularity; really a diaphragm pump is the only sort capable of pumping the shower water reasonably well, without a filter. Once a year the pump will need to be inspected for clogged up pipes and dirty electrical connections; and if the unit is not fitted with a filter it is worth getting one, as it will extend the life of the pump.

A shower drain pump; note the essential filter.

Toilet Systems

Our boating predecessors had some rather barbaric habits when it came to the disposal of human waste: luckily modern boats are better equipped.

The popular and economical caravan toilet has much to recommend it: it can usually be emptied free of charge, it can be stowed in a small compartment, and it is a great improvement on the older 'bucket and chuck it' models; it is easy to clean and relatively smell-free, and the only drawback is that it holds a mere couple of gallons.

'Dump-through' toilets, where a domestic-looking bowl is placed on top of a large waste-holding tank, are also becoming very popular. These systems are designed to be emptied by a large suction pump at a boat-yard; there is usually a fee to pay for this privilege.

There is little to do as regards the mainte-

A 'dump-through' type toilet.

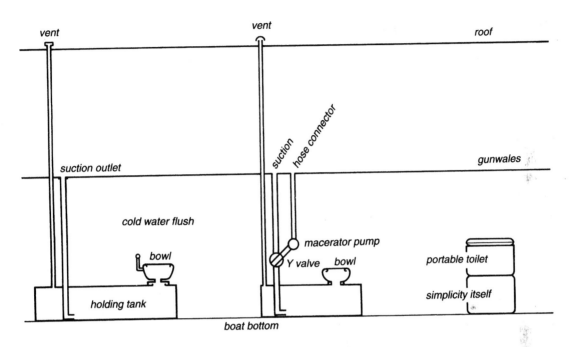

Toilets.

nance of these systems, apart from keeping them clean. A few drops of olive oil on the rubber seals, if they are left for any length of time, will prolong their life. It is a good idea to ensure that none of the sanitary chemicals for the tank come into contact with the seals, since some of these chemicals are rather ferocious in their reactions with organic materials.

Another type of toilet – more commonly found on yachts – has a hand or electric macerator pump which grinds up the waste before pumping it into a holding tank. However, the pumps are vulnerable to blocking, and since the task of stripping them down to remove hard or fibrous debris is a particularly unpleasant chore, they haven't gained great popularity.

Large waste-holding tanks have qualities similar to fresh water tanks: they can be formed as part of the steel shell, or bolted in plastic or stainless steel units. The built-in

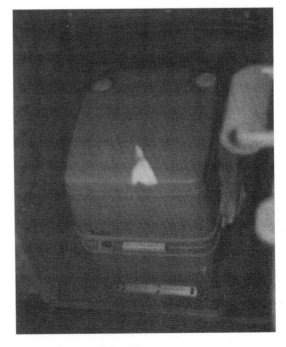

A popular portable toilet.

checked for leaks and rusting clips, in the same way as the sinks. Waste-holding tank systems can be fitted with a second outlet connected to the tank by a 'Y' valve; in this second pipe an electric pump can be fitted so that the boat can pump itself out. A flexible, large diameter pipe is screwed to the second outlet and led to the onshore drain. Cleaning the pipe afterwards is important!

Summary

Like so many other systems in a boat, the initial design and construction of the plumbing system will determine how much maintenance it will require in later years. A well-thought-out layout of pipes, and good quality pumps will mean that the system should be virtually trouble-free. If the system is a bit of a bodge job – and there are plenty of them about – the only sensible solution is to pull the whole lot out and start again. This kind of work is part of a complete refit since it will involve pulling out cupboards and bulkheads.

The importance of the water system is often under-estimated: the health of the whole of the crew is quite dependent on it, since a contaminated water tank will lead to stomach upsets and consequently take the pleasure out of the holiday. Even if you're only using the water for ice in your drink, it is important to keep it clean!

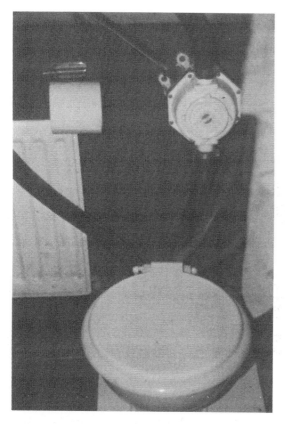

An old-fashioned pump toilet.

tanks are not too prone to rusting, because the waste uses up any oxygen in the air. However, a large tank can upset the boat's stability unless it is placed centrally, and the pipework from the tank needs to be

— 5 —

Heating and Cooking Systems

The heating and cooking systems on a narrow boat vary widely, since the way it is used demands differing qualities and fuels. A boat that is used throughout the year as a residential craft will probably be best suited to a Rayburn or Aga solid fuel stove; it may take a couple of days to get the cooker warm, but since it will be in continuous use this is not a problem. A boat that is used for quick weekend breaks when the weather seems right is more likely to need a gas- or diesel-fired heating and cooking system; there would be no point in trying to fire up a Rayburn for a one-night trip since by the time the thing had got hot the whole cruise would be over!

Ventilation

It is more important to ensure that hot air can get out of a boat, rather than its getting in. A poorly ventilated boat is going to smell rather musty very quickly; the moisture from the occupants will soon start to seep into the wood and rot it, and in the worst cases, the exhaust gases from the cooker and heaters will harm the people inside.

The boat should have been built with plenty of ventilators. They will be set into the door and bulkheads at both floor and ceiling height, and there should be at least one roof vent in each room on the boat. These ventilators do get blocked by dust and cobwebs, and it is worth unscrewing them once a year to clean out any blockages; many have a fine gauze flyscreen incorporated which will need a good scrub. Some surveyors will not approve vents with an integral flyscreen because of their small mesh, and this is unfortunate because the water attracts mosquitos, and flyscreens are an effective way of keeping the little horrors out of the bedroom. If the surveyor refuses to approve of a vent with a screen, a net curtain can always be draped across the door.

If the boat has had extra heating equipment brought on board since its construction, extra vents will need to be fitted to accommodate its demand on the air supply. A surveyor assessing the amount of ventilation in the boat can only count fixed open vents, and it is no good telling him that you will 'open the window whilst dinner is cooking' because he won't believe that you will in the winter.

The boat should have 1sq in (64sq mm) of vent for each person normally on board, a normal two-ring/grill/oven gas cooker will require 30sq in (194sq cm), and a gas water heater will need 6sq in (39sq cm) in addition to the 8sq in (52sq cm) provided by the flue.

Altogether a middle-sized narrow boat should have about 50sq in (323sq cm) of permanently fixed open ventilation, possibly more if there are more appliances. However, it is always worth erring on the side of caution with ventilation, and allowing more vents than are strictly required; if they are properly installed they won't create cold draughts, and their presence will keep the boat smelling clean and fresh.

Ventilation through the interior of the boat is also important. The internal doors and bulkheads need to allow the free flow of air along the cabin, though most boats have so few doors that this is not a problem. The areas that usually suffer from poor air movement are the bathroom and any small cabins set off the main corridor; if these rooms have close-fitting doors it is important to fit ventilators into the top and bottom of them. Louvre doors for bathrooms provide the maximum ventilation whilst maintaining privacy from all but the most inquisitive toddler!

Forced Ventilation

Cooker hoods don't count for much with surveyors, but they do provide an invaluable method of removing the hot, moisture-laden air from the galley. Most contain a foam or paper filter which will need to be cleaned or replaced every so often. Hoods can be awkward to fit after the boat has been built, but they really do help in keeping condensation at bay.

Bilge blowers are not fitted to narrow boats very often. Like cooker hoods, they provide no ventilation when they are not running, but when they are, they suck all the heavy wet air and traces of gas out of the bilges, hopefully keeping them so clean you could eat your dinner out of them! Coaxing the spiders out of the ducts once a year is about all the maintenance they will require.

Windows may appear to provide massive ventilation, but since they can be closed, they can't be counted as part of the fixed vent system.

Gas Systems

Liquid petroleum gas, LPG for short, has been the standard energy source for a long time. It is easy to store and the appliances can provide plenty of heat on demand; the ubiquitous gas-fired water heater can push out over seven kilowatts of heat at the turn of a tap. No other fuel has been able to match this performance. However, LPG has its drawbacks: it has been the biggest single cause of boating tragedies apart from collisions, largely because it is heavier than air and sinks to the bottom of the boat rather than dispersing. It is explosive and can be ignited by a stray spark, so if a gas leak does happen on a boat, the consequences can be fatal.

There is now a whole list of regulations that an LPG system has to meet: nor does it really matter if your boat is a venerable and ancient craft, because the gas system must meet the most up-to-date specifications. These new regulations have had many, if not most, boaters muttering darkly about the interference of ignorant pen-pushers, but the sad truth is that if the current rules had been in force all along, there would be more boaters alive now.

Although the installation of LPG systems might appear to be within the capabilities of most handymen, there are fine nuances to the system design which have to be incorporated. The most important of these is the pressure drop along the pipe length. The gas in the pipe encounters friction from the pipe walls and bends, and this results in a pressure drop when a large volume of gas is drawn off. A small drop merely reduces the operating efficiency of the appliance, but a larger drop can have serious repercussions. Thus calculating the right pipe size is more than just guessing that it looked okay on the other boats you have seen – there are many boats that have gas pipes which are too small for the volume they are expected to carry. Even the much maligned Certificate of Compliance is no guarantee that the LPG system will pass a pressure-drop test.

Gas Central Heating

There are several makes of water- and central-

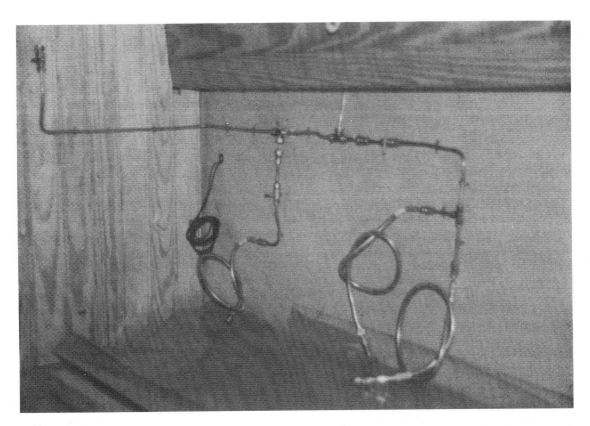

A new gas system.

heating boilers that run extremely well on narrow boats and which have been proven over years of use to withstand life on board and provide trouble-free heating, provided they are correctly serviced. In normal use they should require little attention apart from a check that the flame is burning with the correct coloured flame, and any particular instruction mentioned in the individual manual. In the event of a boiler failing, switch off the gas supply and call an engineer.

Gas Bottles

The size of the gas bottle determines the amount of gas that can be drawn from it, both in overall quantity and in cubic feet per minute. The gas inside the bottle is a liquid

Cobwebs inside the gas rings can cause the flames to burn yellow instead of the correct blue colour.

*Bottles stored on deck need to be
secured.*

under pressure; when an appliance is used,
the pressure in the pipework drops and the
regulator allows gas from the top of the bottle
to flow into the pipe. This means the pressure
in the bottle will drop, so some of the liquid
gas evaporates to build the pressure up again;
it requires heat to evaporate, which it draws
in through the bottle walls. In a well-
balanced system this is hardly noticeable.

If the gas system has been designed poorly
and the bottles are too small, the heat needed
to evaporate the liquid simply cannot be conducted through the bottle walls fast enough.
A clear symptom of this is the formation of
ice on the bottle, and it can lead to an overall
pressure drop through the gas system.

Most boats are built with lockers that will
take 13-kilo propane cylinders. These are big
enough to cope with all but the largest
central-heating systems. If your gas locker
can only take the small cylinders you will
have to be careful how many gas appliances
you run.

Gas Lockers

Gas lockers tend to become unofficial glory-
holes containing all sorts of boating junk as
well as the gas bottles. This isn't very good
practice. The vents that allow any spilt gas to
drain overboard can be blocked by some stray
bit of rag, and this would negate the safety
aspect which should be provided by the
locker. It is worth keeping lockers clean and
free of things that could block the vents.

Some gas lockers have to be so deep to
accommodate the bottles that their base is
under the water-line; the vents at the bottom
then allow the water into the locker, and can
prevent the surplus gas escaping. This is
partly the result of poor planning by the boat
builder, and partly because the rules about
gas storage have changed over the lifetime of
the boat. It is important that there is a vent
open to the air, even if this means drilling a
second vent just above the water-line.

This problem has other consequences.
Being the junk-yards that they are, gas lockers tend to be overlooked in a boat's painting
schedule, and rust quietly away. If the base of
the locker is below the water-line, this can
have serious consequences, even to the point
of sinking the boat! A good clean-out once a
year is therefore worthwhile. Further, the
inside of a gas locker takes a lot more
scratches than virtually any other part of the
boat: lugging heavy cylinders into a confined
space, dropping windlasses, lump hammers
and mooring spikes in there as well, all wear
the paint away and let the rust take hold. The
inside of the locker will last better if it is
painted with an impact-resistant paint, and a
wooden board or slats along the bottom will
help, too.

Gas Refrigeration

For many years a certain make of gas fridge
has been fitted into boats and has worked
perfectly satisfactorily. However, the manu-

Gas lockers should be uncluttered!

facturers still refuse to recommend that the fridge is suitable for use on boats – the problem lies, in fact, in the very nature of gas-powered fridges, which work on the 'absorption' principle; the workings inside are complicated and depend on the unit being mounted upright. Very basically, a small gas flame heats an ammonia solution to produce ammonia gas which behaves in a way similar to an ordinary fridge, except that it returns to a water solution before being reheated to circulate once more. The delicate balance of gas to solution is dependent on the level of the unit, and a tilt of more than 6° will upset the working of the thing. The manufacturer probably has visions of hardy narrow-boaters bravely crossing the North Atlantic in winter, and so remains adamant about not recommending them for boats.

The exposed pilot light of the gas fridge is also a bone of contention amongst surveyors. If it blows out it could release gas into the cabin; alight it could ignite gas from other gas leaks. Installing these fridges to meet a surveyor's approval can be tricky and is best discussed with the surveyor in advance. If there is already one fitted in your boat, make sure you keep the ventilation grills above and below it clean, and any vents through the hull should be inspected regularly for obstructions.

The regulations about these fridges have become so complicated that most boat builders are now using electrically-operated units; these work on exactly the same principle, only use a little electric heating element instead of the pilot light. It is still important to check the vents are clean. The electric versions of the absorption fridge do use a fair bit of power from the battery, and it is a good idea to check the electrolyte levels once a week whilst the unit is in use.

CORGI Inspection

The maintenance of the gas system has now become a task that needs to be carried out by a professional gas fitter. It is important that the system is inspected at least once a year, and if necessary have the chimney flues swept out, the burners cleaned and a pressure drop test as well. Most boat-yards are now employing gas fitters, and can call on CORGI-registered inspectors to give any system a clean bill of health.

User Inspection

There are certain points that you can exam-

Gas Pipe Diameter Guide			
Appliance	Distance from cylinder in metres		
	0–5	5–10	10–20
Fridge	1/4"	3/8"	1/2"
2 ring cooker	3/8"	1/2"	5/8"
Full size cooker	1/2"	1"	1"
Water Heater	1/2"	1"	1"
Full Size Cooker and water heater and fridge	1/2"	1"	1"

Note that the number of bends and connections will alter the gas flow characteristics in the pipework. Every system should be inspected by a qualified fitter.

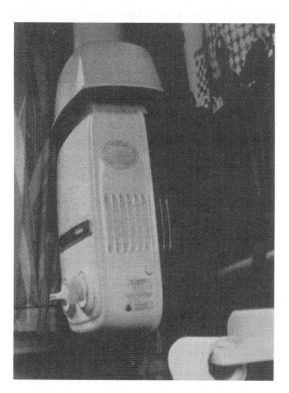

It is possible to fit certain water heaters without shortening the flue.

ine. The pipe diameter from the gas regulator to the cooker and water heater should be a minimum of 10mm (3/8in) if it is a short length, of less than 3m (10ft); for a longer boat 12mm (1/2in) is the smallest practical size. There are plenty of boats with smaller pipe than this, and if yours is one of them you should start discussing alterations with a gas fitter.

There is a pressure gauge available which screws into the system between the gas cylinder and the regulator, marketed as a means of assessing the amount of gas left in the cylinder and as a leak detector. In practice the gauge is difficult to use to assess the cylinder contents, because the temperature and flow rate vary so widely that accuracy is impossible, but it does have a very useful role in detecting leaks. It can be used every time the gas bottle is turned off. Since gas pipes can fracture after a few years of vibration in a boat, especially if they were over-tightened on installation, an on-going leak tester like this is a worthwhile addition to the system. Apart from changing the gas cylinder, there is not much else that the non-qualified operator can do!

Solid Fuel

Coal-fired stoves are perfect for narrow boats: they can provide enough heat to make the boat as warm as toast on the coldest day of the year; they can also be fitted with a back boiler to heat radiators along the boat, as well as the hot water system. Multifuel stoves will run on just about anything inflammable – the junk that clutters the towpath, forklift-truck pallets and dead branches can all be chopped up and used for heat – but they do not like burning bituminous coal because the high tar content of the smoke clogs up the chimney and reduces its efficiency. Ordinary anthracite coals burn bright and clean, without

Solid fuel stoves need a good fire regularly to keep the chimney clean.

leaving too much tar dribbling down the inside of the flue. The stoves need to be kept clean, particularly the air vents into the grate and the flue.

The whole canal system was virtually dedicated to coal transport in its early years: quite a lot must have fallen off the boats and it is still possible to pick enough coal out of dredgings and the towpath edge to run a stove. It smokes rather badly but still burns.

Safety

Solid fuel stoves need to be securely mounted in the boat; a close encounter with a lock or bridge could knock them over, spreading embers all over the floor. The nature of the stove means that its sides will be very hot, so with children on board, a fire guard should be deployed to prevent them touching what appears to be an ordinary black surface; they are not to know that it is several hundred degrees. Finally, a clear unobstructed chimney is of primary importance – no one wants toxic smoke pervading the air inside, particularly if you are asleep.

Central Heating from Solid Fuel

Most small solid fuel stoves have a back boiler which can run two or three small radiators and a second coil in the calorifier. A heating engineer would say that this wasn't possible, because the stoves simply do not have the output in British thermal units. In practice they do, as the low output of the stoves allows a gravity circulation to operate, naturally circulating the hot water around the system by convection. The system should be frost-protected, which means antifreeze. Large-bore copper pipes are essential to the working of a gravity system and have to be protected.

The stove can also be used to heat the water supply. A twin-coil calorifier has one heating coil driven from the engine and one from the

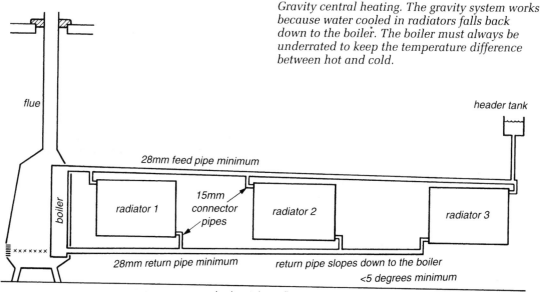

Gravity central heating. The gravity system works because water cooled in radiators falls back down to the boiler. The boiler must always be underrated to keep the temperature difference between hot and cold.

flue

header tank

28mm feed pipe minimum

boiler

radiator 1

15mm connector pipes

radiator 2

radiator 3

28mm return pipe minimum

return pipe slopes down to the boiler
<5 degrees minimum

horizontal; not floor

Gravity-fed radiator.

stove; this will need a second pipe-run from the stove, and quite possibly a pump. A gravity feed to the coil is less likely to work well and needs the pump.

Looking after this sort of system isn't difficult. The header tank for the radiators should be inspected every few weeks to make sure there is no loss of the circulating fluid from evaporation. The antifreeze mix should be changed every couple of years, and the circulating pump checked each year for clean electrical contacts. If the system is used to heat the hot water it is normal practice in the heating industry to use a non-toxic antifreeze; this is to prevent contamination of the potable water in the event of a failure of the heating coil in the calorifier. This should apply to the engine's coolant system too, although it isn't often done!

The great advantage of a gravity-powered heating system is that is uses no electricity; this makes it very suitable for residential boats without mains power.

Diesel-fired Heating Systems

Narrow boats already have a large fuel tank on board, and it makes good sense to use this fuel store to power the heating system. Diesel oil is not the most suitable fuel oil for heating purposes as the lighter heating oil burns more efficiently, but since the latter won't run a generator or an engine so well a compromise has to be made.

As the gas regulations have become more and more stringent, boat builders have moved away from using LPG; this has led to the installation of diesel-fired boilers and even cookers, which have proved themselves to be a very useful alternative. There are many different types. Some boilers rely on an electrical blower and pump to atomize the fuel and force the flame through a heat exchanger, others allow the oil to drip onto a preheated plate and burn the resulting evaporated oil. Diesel evaporates at a higher temperature than ordinary heating oil, and so the design of these units is quite critical.

Each boiler will need to be looked after according to its own instruction manual, though they all need a plentiful supply of air, and a free and unobstructed flue, just like a solid fuel stove. The boilers are not quite as fussy about the fuel oil's cleanliness as an engine, but they will need a filter in their supply pipe, and this will need changing each year. Water-contaminated fuel can cause intermittent faults and unexpected breakdowns.

The heating systems run from a diesel boiler can be more ambitious than those run from a solid fuel stove because the power output is much greater. The boilers are usually very compact in size, especially the electrically-driven ones, and can be fitted into a corner of an engine compartment.

Diesel-fuelled cookers used to have a reputation for being smelly and smoky; modern ones however are directly comparable to gas, apart from needing a slightly longer warm-up time. For anyone who despairs of getting a gas system correctly installed in a boat, these new cookers have become available at just the right time.

Summary

There is a wide range of appliances to provide heat for a narrow boat, ranging from the simple and inexpensive to sophisticated, thermostat-controlled central-heating systems. Each of the fuel systems, whether gas, oil or solid fuel, has its own safety requirements and these must be adhered to at all costs. If a system has been properly installed, its maintenance requirements will be easy to follow; in the case of gas systems, this will allow the engineer to inspect and service it easily, thus reducing his labour costs.

Although the imposition of ever more stringent controls on gas systems has increased the cost of maintenance for the boat owner, there are valid reasons for this emphasis on safety. In particular it is the duty of the boat owner to ensure the safety of everyone on board.

— 6 —

Woodwork and Fitting Out

The interior of most narrow boats is a complex mixture of traditional carpentry, modern appliances, upholstery and interior design. A boat contains virtually all the features of a house, usually designed and planned in much more detail. It is somewhat more compact, too!

Like a house, the elements, time and wear all conspire to reduce the boat to a shambles. Dry and wet rot can wreck the woodwork, even woodworm has been known to make a meal of someone's pride and joy. Damp air encourages the growth of moulds on fabrics, and mud from the towpath can quickly destroy the carpets. All in all, the maintenance of a boat's interior can seem like an uphill struggle.

Interior Woodwork

There is a wide selection of timber available for the boat builder to use, particularly as in recent years plywoods faced with ornamental woods have become more widely available, and relatively cheap, too; when the first leisure narrow boats were built in the early sixties there was only a very restricted range of cabin lining materials available, tongue-and-groove pine being the most commonly used. Many boats were finished with melamine-surfaced hardboard, which has proved to be easy to clean but poor at withstanding the damp; chipboard has also proved to be a short-lived material in boats. Marine- and exterior-grade plywoods seem to have stood the test of time well, and the new,

exotically-faced plywoods should have a good lifespan, although they are only an interior grade.

It does seem a somewhat short-sighted policy to manufacture a beautiful piece of plywood whose good face is made of cherry wood, oak or even teak, and then use an interior grade glue to stick the sheets together, but this is the way it has been done. These woods really do look stunning in a boat, but to keep them at their best it is important to ensure the boat is well ventilated. A good initial coat of preservative, and then varnish, regularly maintained, will also help to maintain their beauty for a long time.

Most bulkheads and the walls inside a boat are made from a thick sheet of block-board; this is rugged and strong unless an interior grade has been used, in which case very damp air will gradually destroy the adhesive holding it together, and one day it will start to come apart. If you can take the piece out before it disintegrates it will be useful as a template for a new piece.

The structural timbers beneath the floor and supporting the lining are often made of hardwood, oak being the most popular for the floor bearers. After about ten years these will benefit from a brush-over with some more preservative – although most of their surfaces will be inaccessible, so there is only so much that can be treated. The timbers behind the cladding are also virtually impossible to reach, and so one has to hope that the boat builder used a really good wood preserver to start with.

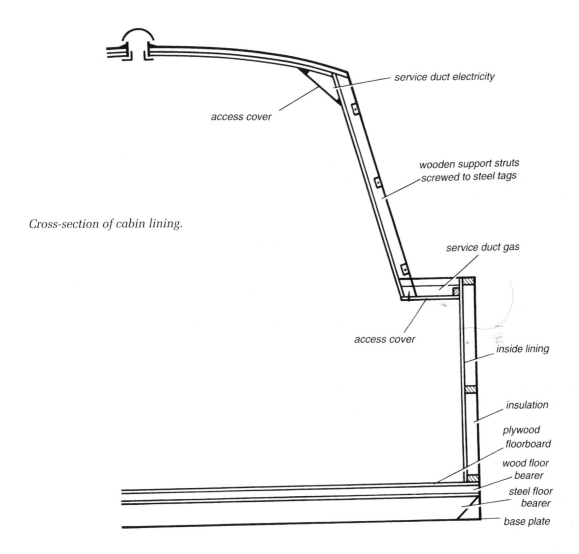

Cross-section of cabin lining.

service duct electricity

access cover

wooden support struts
screwed to steel tags

service duct gas

access cover

inside lining

insulation

plywood
floorboard

wood floor
bearer

steel floor
bearer

base plate

Protecting the Woodwork

The inside of a boat is almost entirely constructed from wood so bulkheads, floors and
walls are all susceptible to attack by insects
and rot. Whilst the boat is under construction
it is important to treat all wood liberally with
a long-lasting wood preserver, a process
which should keep any potential damage at
bay for at least ten years, and longer if the
wood can be well maintained.

Wood Rots

Ensuring that the ventilation system is in
good working order is the best way of keeping the woodwork free of rot. Wet rot will take
advantage of any places where the wood
remains constantly damp, darkening the
colour and destroying its strength, and
despite its name, dry rot also favours a humid
environment. This starts with a certain dis-
coloration of the wood which gets worse, the

Ventilators are vitally important.

wood then starts to break up into cubes about an inch square, and finally a foul-smelling fungal growth develops – there is no mistaking the ultimate stage of dry rot, a large brown mat of fungus spreading white filaments across the wood. If it has got this far it constitutes a very serious problem indeed.

The severity of the damage will determine just how much remedial action is required. A patch of wet rot can be treated without too much upheaval, but the most important aspect of any treatment is to ascertain the cause of the rot. Wet rot is almost invariably started by the constant presence of water, and a frequent cause of this is a leaking window or roof fitting. The water drips onto the wood, and if there is poor ventilation it will become permanently saturated; rot will inevitably set in under these circumstances. So first fix the leak. The extent of the rot then needs to be established, and the damaged material removed for at least twelve inches beyond the obvious edge of the softened wood. The whole area needs to be treated with a preser-

vative and fungicide, including the steel which can harbour the spores in its crevices. The new wood also needs to be thoroughly soaked in preservative.

If the area affected is extensive it may well include structural items like bulkheads and floor bearers. It is important to replace these items with new ones that will be able to take the loads imposed on them. If the bottom six inches of a bulkhead have been rotted away, examine the loads that the wood is bearing before you cut anything out; cupboards or cookers may be supported by this piece, and it may transpire that the work is a lot more complicated than it first appears.

Dry rot is the real nightmare for boats: it is prevalent in areas close to the sea, and coastal and estuary craft are often riddled with it. Narrow boats on the whole don't suffer as badly, but when they do the remedial work can be extensive. Dry rot is an insidious fungus. The early stages can be difficult to recognize, and if the fungus has got a grip, treatment has to be drastic. As for wet rot, wet wood provides a food source, and stagnant humid air allows the microscopic filaments to spread; the fungus will pervade deep into the tissue of the wood, absorbing moisture and nutrients from it. As the attack progresses the wood appears to dry out and crack up into cubes, and the filaments travel further away from the initial infection seeking more food. Eventually the fungus decides to reproduce and forms a fruiting body to scatter spores into the air; the fruit body is like a brown and white mat. The fungus has a very distinctive smell and if you are familiar with it you will be alerted before major damage is caused.

If the fungus is recognized early enough, the cure doesn't have to be too drastic. However, all the infected wood has to be removed, and this does mean that apparently good wood must go too because the filaments can spread up to a yard from the edge of the visible infection; even a few cells left behind will be enough for the rot to start growing again. Dry rot is not that discriminating, either, and the filaments will grow into everything looking for food, including the insulation, carpets and steel – though they might not get far into the steel. Thus all the materials that are in close proximity but cannot be removed must be treated with a strong fungicide, too, as must all the new material brought in to replace the damage.

At the same time as this repair work is being carried out, the entire boat will need to be examined for other outbreaks. The most common troublespots are the floor bearers in the bilges, dark damp cupboards in the bathroom, and the wood around leaky hatches and windows. An extra treatment with preservative as you look will help to control further outbreaks, and the ventilation should be examined to make sure it is working properly.

In the event of a very bad outbreak of dry rot, the only practical solution may be to strip out all the woodwork inside the boat and refit the entire craft. As you can imagine, it is worth destroying the fungus before this becomes necessary.

Woodworm

Woodworm and death-watch beetle don't usually offer a serious threat to boats, but they can cause unsightly damage. Once the initial wood treatment has worn off, it is a matter of keeping a sharp eye on all the woodwork; if the tell-tale holes appear, a squirt of woodworm killer into them should keep the little horrors under control.

It is possible to treat all the wood with a woodworm killer if the attack is serious. The process is best done when the boat is out of commission in the winter because the chemicals that kill the insects are rather toxic and very persistent, and the boat will want several month's airing after treatment. It is also just as well to check that none of the crew is allergic to the sprays before using them,

because once the boat has been sprayed it will aggravate an allergy for several years. There is a considerable choice of woodworm killers, so you should be able to find one that will suit your needs.

Varnish

Narrow boats have a wealth of wood inside them, including tropical hardwoods and Canadian redwoods, and all serve to make the interior a warm and inviting living space. Their real beauty is enhanced and prolonged by the application of varnish. When the boat is built it is treated with wood preserver and varnish: the preservative should last for ten or fifteen years, and even longer if the chemicals are trapped into the wood by an effective varnish coat.

Varnish will prevent the sunlight fading the wood colours, it will enhance the contrast of the different grains, and most importantly it will prevent those grubby finger-marks penetrating into the wood fibres. To keep a surface looking at its best, a wipe down with a damp cloth every now and then will keep it clean. After a few years, however, the build-up of scratches will have dulled the finish and the boat will be looking slightly shabby: a fresh coat of varnish can transform the interior. The woodwork will need to be prepared by washing all the surface dirt off, and very lightly removing the top layer of the existing varnish with a fine grade of emery paper. All the dust resulting from this must be removed – plenty of fresh air circulating through the boat helps – and a fresh coat can then be applied. This will be enough to bring the shine back!

If you are an absolute perfectionist another sanding and another coat should give such a brilliant finish you could use the wood as a shaving mirror. I know one person who polishes the hardened varnish with metal polish to achieve a surface so smooth it would probably work as a telescope mirror!

Fittings and Furnishings

Furniture and Appliances

Most boats have a selection of furniture which doesn't usually need much attention. The fixed cupboards and shelves will need a clean every so often, though that is when they show up a common design flaw: boat shelves have to be built with a raised lip, or 'Fiddle-stick', as a guard against the vibration shaking the priceless Staffordshire pottery off the shelf and onto the floor. However, the raised lip needs to have a gap in it so the dust can be wiped off, otherwise it simply accumulates in the corner and the shelf never looks clean. The gap only needs to be a couple of inches long, and it it isn't there to start with, a bit of careful work with a coping saw or Stanley knife will resolve the dust-trap problem.

There are enough appliances on board for it to be worthwhile to take the time to check them all methodically. Gas fires, fridges and cookers must all be securely fastened down; in the event of a collision, you don't want the situation made worse by the cooker flying around and setting fire to the curtains. Nuts and bolts do have a way of working loose when you're not looking, so physically check them with a spanner. Ideally the appliances should be fastened with stainless steel bolts with lock-nuts; this way you can be sure that the job has been done properly. It is most important that any solid fuel stoves are securely bolted down.

Electrical appliances don't normally create such a hazard if they come loose, although they are still worth checking since short-circuits can cause fires. Showers and sinks aren't going to set the boat alight if they work loose, they will simply let water get into places where it shouldn't be; nevertheless this encourages wood rots, so check that they are firm, and that the sealant around the edge of any bath or shower tray is intact.

Hinges, Drawers and Beds

There is an assortment of moving furniture and fittings on a boat that will need some attention every so often. For example, hinges on the cupboards and doors are usually made of brass, which doesn't rust away like steel but is soft and needs a drop of oil to prevent wear. Brass also needs a polish to stay looking bright. Once it is polished, a wipe over with an oily cloth keeps the brightness for longer; Vaseline or any light oil will do the trick. It can be lacquered or varnished to maintain its polish, too, although if the job isn't done well a mottled pattern of tarnish will develop and look ten times worse than if you had just left it alone.

Plastic drawer runners seem to go on forever without any attention, though wooden runners can become stiff if they aren't lubricated. Beeswax makes an ideal lubricant; simply rub a stick of wax over the sliding surfaces. Ordinary candle-wax does as well, but doesn't smell half as homely. Sliding leaves on tables and beds also benefit from a rub of beeswax on their runners. Most boats use demountable legs; these are versatile and strong, simply slotting into the floor socket and, say, table to make a surprisingly rigid support. It is getting them unslotted that can be a problem: the more weight the support takes, the harder the leg is forced into its socket. The sockets and tapered end need to be kept free of grit, and a wipe with a light oil will help prevent them becoming so tightly engaged that it takes all your strength to demount them.

Fabrics and Upholstery

The soft furnishings of the boat should be flameproofed when they are fitted, to help prevent the spread of any fire. There are, however, a lot of boats that were built before the introduction of modern fire-retardant foams and materials, and even when the regulations about using these new foams in household furniture were brought into force, it took some time for boat builders to follow suit. There is, therefore, a potential killer on board many boats since the non-fire-retardant foam burns very easily, and liberates dense poisonous smoke as it does so. It is well worth examining the cushions on your boat to make sure it is safe.

The new flame-retardant foams are generally blue or green whilst the older, more dangerous ones are a cream colour. This is not a hard and fast rule, and if you have the slightest doubt about the foam, take a small sample out of the cushion and try to burn it (outside the boat). If it refuses to burn and just melts into a mess there is no problem; but if it burns easily, giving off a noxious black smoke, imagine what it would be like if you were inside the boat when a whole cushion was on fire! New cushions need not be too expensive if you shop around.

Stretch sofa and chair covers are usually manufactured with a flame-retardant additive; if they need a clean, it is worth taking them to a dry cleaners and specifying that they have to *remain fire-retardant*. Curtains tend to require more washing, and can be treated with a spray-on flame retarder once they have been dried.

Carpets made of plastics can be another fire risk; the old-fashioned wool and hessian ones will burn gradually, but not with the intense heat and smoke of artificial fibres.

Fire Extinguishers

Extinguishers are the first line of defence against fire and it is most important to have ones of good quality that meet all the legal requirements. The only time you will want to use them is when there is a fire on board, and that will not be a suitable time to go and buy better ones; so do make sure that you have the

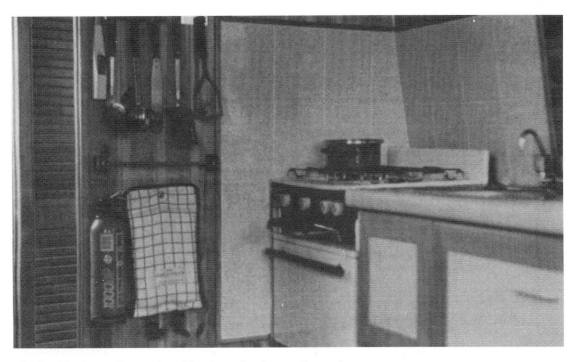

The fire blanket and an extinguisher must be close to the cooker.

best on board. Fire extinguishers have a short life-span, and there is a date printed on them after which they cannot be considered as reliable. Good quality extinguishers are expensive, but if they prevent your boat being burnt out the cost is negligible.

Out-of-date extinguishers provide a valuable chance actually to use the things, particularly as they can be returned to the manufacturer for recharging for less than the cost of a new one, in most cases. Before they go, why not try one out? You needn't set the boat on fire, of course, but if you are having a bonfire at the bottom of the garden, try and put it out. You may find that the capacity of a fire extinguisher is not as great as you expected – and you may also find that the mess a dry powder extinguisher makes is much greater! However, the practice will be of value if ever you need to use one in an emergency.

Dry powder extinguishers are the type most used, containing a white powder which has powerful fire-extinguishing properties; this is propelled out of the canister by pressurized nitrogen gas. Every extinguisher has a gauge on it to show whether it is adequately pressurized, and should be examined at least once a year to ensure that the pressure is correct; at the same time it should be given a shake to prevent the powder in it from becoming compacted in the bottom.

Carbon dioxide and halon extinguishers are not the best ones for use in a boat because they exclude the oxygen from the people as well as the fire.

The fire blanket by the cooker shouldn't need any maintenance, but do check that small children haven't pulled it out, leaving only the container hanging on the wall!

Insects

Spiders and woodlice are keen boaters. Woodlice are in fact a symptom of damp wood in the boat, as are silverfish, and the best way to keep them out is to make sure that the boat is dry; then the spiders will feel more at home. Spiders build their webs in the most peculiar, and occasionally dangerous places, the worst being the gas cooker: if the web obstructs the flow of gas between the gas jet and the ring, a poorly ventilated flame will result; this will be a yellow colour, and will quite probably issue from the jet. If this happens, turn off the gas immediately and call in a qualified gas engineer to clean the burners.

Spiders also build their webs in the ventilation holes in the gas locker which would prevent gas escaping, and in the ordinary ventilators thus preventing the free flow of air; a quick whisk with a duster rectifies this. They climb inside cassette players, too, and get mashed up into the tape, which does little for the quality of sound reproduction! A tape-head cleaning tape will help. No one knows why spiders are so keen on boats; I was watching the launch of a bare shell once, and the boat had been in the water no more than a minute when I spotted a spider rushing up the mooring line, intent on moving in. In fact, spiders are generally a good sign that the boat is dry inside, and that bodes well for the longevity of the fabric. My wife disagrees intensely.

Refitting

Older boats eventually reach a stage where they need quite major work on them, and a partial or total refit is effectively the only way to solve a serious backlog of wear and tear; however, if the refit is planned well in advance this shouldn't be a problem. If you don't feel that your carpentry skills are good enough, there are plenty of boat fitters who will be able to do the work. In either case you will need to sit down and work out exactly what the boat needs: a written list of the items that need to be replaced is essential in order to negotiate a price with a boat fitter.

Some refits can take years!

When refitting a boat it is best to go back to square one.

Besides, it is a good idea to get several quotes from different builders, and you can only compare their prices if they are all quoting for the same work.

A refit involves virtually the same work as that done when the boat is first fitted out; when extensive work becomes necessary on one part of the structure, the other parts might as well be renewed as well. If you were to replace all the walls and ceilings, but left the wiring, you might find that a year later the new wood had to be removed to repair a broken wire ('Murphy's Law', meaning that no matter how short the wire run behind the cladding is, that's where it will break!). In most cases the refit process is best tackled

Where it all started, a boatman's cabin on a butty.

from the bare steel – and even the steel will need at least a new coat of paint.

There are several important considerations to take into account if you intend to do the work yourself: Quite apart from your ability actually to do the work to a standard that a surveyor will judge safe, this type of work takes time. Most boats that are refitted take two years before they are back in working order, and some take a lot longer, or are never finished. A general guide is that the project will take twice as long as expected, and cost twice as much.

The structure of the hull is important, as there is no point in spending a lot of hard-earned money on refitting a hull that promptly sinks. A thorough survey of the hull plate thicknesses by a marine surveyor is essential – it may cost a hundred pounds, but it could save you pouring thousands into a white elephant.

A refit allows much more than just a major repairing session, which is just as well, since a boat that is twenty years old may well have a different purpose now than it did at first. The children may have grown up, left the nest and bought their own boats, leaving several unoccupied berths; more children might have arrived, needing more berths than were originally built. A refit will allow the entire interior lay-out to be redesigned to suit your current needs. The ways that boat builders have worked out as to how to live in a seven-foot wide corridor have also changed over the years, and many new boats are a revelation in ways to squeeze a quart into a pint pot.

When the old timbers and fittings have been stripped out, they can usually be sold to someone building his first boat on a very tight budget; this will help to defray the cost of the new work, and help him get onto the water within his budget. 'Boat-boot' sales occur every so often, and can represent a good way of converting a garage full of redundant boat bits into cash. They are also pretty handy for getting equipment cheap if you have to.

Refitting a boat is a major task.

much higher than before. The use of modern, ornamental-faced plywoods and the consistent use of stainless steel fastenings will push up the cost of the work, but the longevity of the boat will be greatly enhanced. At least this time the cost of the hull doesn't have to be taken into account.

Summary

The interior of a boat is a complex mixture of fine woods and complicated fittings. Cruising on the canals means that mud and grass tend to be brought into the boat on a regular basis, and cleanliness is vital to keep the boat looking good. Ventilation is also essential to ensure the long life of the interior. When all is said and done, the boat is a vehicle and this means that the fixtures and fittings are prone to damage from vibration, and must be checked regularly.

At this juncture the boat will be in the optimum state to have any major welding work carried out, nor is it that expensive or difficult to have the boat stretched. This will involve getting the boat into a dry dock or boat-yard, cutting it in half, and welding an extra length of hull in the middle. The expensive parts of the boat are the bow and stern swims; the bit in the middle is no more complicated than a rubbish skip to fabricate. You will need quotes from several different boat builders to assess the best value on offer.

The plan for the refit should really wait until you have had a chance to examine as many new boats as you can. Boat rallies and shows will provide an excellent opportunity for you to see the latest ideas, and these can then be incorporated into your plan.

The specification of the refitted craft can be

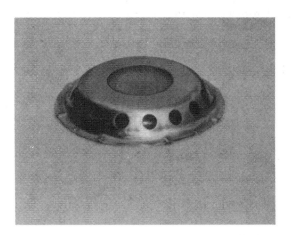

Cruiser-style ventilator.

The nature of narrow boats means that they can be extensively refitted when the interior becomes worn out. This will preserve the initial investment for decades, and possibly even generations. That's not something you can say for many other vehicles!

— 7 —

Paperwork and Safety

One of the main reasons for having a boat is to get away from all the paperwork and telephones that besiege everyday life. A day's relaxing cruising along a willow-lined sunlit canal washes away the cares generated by a pile of bills and harassed phone calls. The catch is that when you get home they are still there, and even the boat will generate some of its own paperwork. Insurance, mooring fees, bills of sale and the Boat Safety Certificate – gradually even the relaxed atmosphere of the canals is becoming hedged about with paper walls.

The documents and certificates required for narrow boats aren't quite as bad as for a car, but it is still important to keep them all in order. In years to come the European Union will generate even more paperwork, as is its nature, and no doubt there will be enforcement policies to ensure that us poor boaters toe the line!

Buying a Boat

Narrow boats are expensive – some have a price tag well in excess of that of a detached house – and it is important to ensure that that cost is protected by following a proper legal procedure. In much the same way that the maintenance costs of the engine are determined by the quality of its installation, the costs and problems of owning a boat can be greatly affected by the initial effort put into the purchase. The boat may be new or secondhand, big or small, but the paperwork surrounding the sale has to be in order.

New Boats

At long last the beat-up old wreck that you bought for a song twenty years ago is either falling to bits or is just too small to take the whole family on board at once. You decide to invest in a nice new boat; and, having recovered from the shock of the prices, find a boat builder to make it for you. Just finding a builder can take months, but it will undoubtedly pay dividends to spend plenty of time on this stage of the business. You will need to draw up a plan and written specification of the boat you want; every boat is custombuilt, so builders won't be surprised if you turn up with sheets of graph paper and lists of equipment. These plans will form the basis of a contract between you and the builder, and also the information on which he will base his price for the job. If your plans are a hastily scrawled note on the back of an envelope, his quote will probably be the same, and you can then spend several years and thousands of pounds arguing out the omitted details in court. This will make your solicitor a lot richer, but won't get you onto the water.

A proper contract between you and the boat builder is a written document which describes in detail the boat that you want built, and the detail is very important: the more complicated the boat, the longer the document will need to be. It must include the price which you have agreed with the builder, and the delivery date; and it will need to detail any deposits, stage payments and guarantees as well. If you are in any doubt at all, go and ask a solicitor or the legal

A clear specification will allow the builder to make a first-class boat.

adviser at the Citizens Advice Bureau. Since boats are so expensive it is very important to get this part of the business correct.

A written plan will enable you to get an assortment of quotes from different builders; there is not much point in asking ten builders to quote on ten different plans, as you won't be able to make a comparison. On the whole the principle of 'You get what you pay for' is true, but there are one or two notable exceptions and some builders provide an extremely high quality build for a surprisingly low price, whilst others charge a fortune for a very shoddy boat. As you comb the countryside for boat builders, make a point of examining boats that builders are in the process of constructing to see if their quality seems to match the price.

Once you have found a builder you like – which is very important – and who is close enough for you to keep a regular watch on the progress of construction, you will have to provide him with a written order for the boat, as detailed in your plans. He will also want a deposit. Some builders ask for huge deposits, sometimes even the whole price in advance; however, 10 per cent is reasonable, and if he needs more than this you should ask yourself why – the answer may be that he hasn't enough capital to buy the steel or fittings, and if he hasn't got that much there's a risk that he might go bankrupt before he has finished building the boat. If that happens you will end up losing both deposit and boat.

Some builders work on a stage payment scheme. When the shell is complete, you buy it from him, and he then uses his profit from that to fund the next stage of the fit-out; and when that is paid for, the engine goes in. This is a reasonable way to do things as long as you

New boat under construction.

Boat building is a cooperative venture between the builder and buyer.

get proper legal title to the boat at each stage of the construction; then if the receivers are called in to wind up the business, the boat is your property and they can't auction it off. You may lose some money and have to have another builder to finish the job, but it won't be a catastrophe.

The completion stage of a new boat is usually when all the arguments occur. If you have specified a detail in writing such as teak tables and the builder has put in walnut, you can insist that he alters it. In such a case you may decide that the builder has done a better job than you specified, but if he then adds a couple of hundred pounds to the bill you can refuse to pay it. It is this sort of diversion from the specification that creates most of the arguments, but if you can keep a close eye on the construction you will be able to spot any such deviations before the builder has invested too much time and money on them. If you don't feel qualified to pass judgement on the boat as it is being built, you can always employ a surveyor to check the con-

struction a couple of times. It is an extra expense, but it might save you a lot of trouble later on.

Once all the haggling about the fittings is over, the boat should be ready for delivery. It should come with a 'Boat Safety Certificate', which means it has been surveyed by an expert and meets all the current safety rules fully (for these rules in detail see p. 110–25). In much the same way that an MOT for a car does not cover everything, neither does the certificate and it shouldn't be taken to mean that the boat is in perfect working order; you will need to go over it with a fine toothcomb yourself and check that everything is correctly installed and working. And then there is always the nagging suspicion that if *you* can do this check, you are probably quite capable of building the boat yourself and saving a fortune!

The builder should have put together a manual explaining all the systems on board and their maintenance; there should be a written guarantee covering the boat, or at least the engine; there will be a bill of sale specifying what the boat is, who has built it and who has bought it, together with any registration and security numbers; and lastly there is the receipt for payment. One might hope that you will then be able to cruise off into the sunset with never another problem. However, it doesn't always work out this way, and flaws in the paperwork can trip you up. The most common trouble is the engine installation: the engine fails, the boat builder then blames the manufacturer, who insists that the installation was incorrect, and they both deny liability. The boat owner is reduced to bow-hauling in order to get anywhere. Make sure the paperwork specifies whose responsibility the engine is, and then this sort of trouble can be avoided.

Secondhand Boats

It is much easier to buy a secondhand boat: you find the boat that suits your needs, and haggle over the price, and buy it. To do this properly you will need to look at dozens, if not hundreds of boats until you find the best one, and you will then want to take it for a short test cruise to check how it handles; most boats handle perfectly well forwards but some, if not most, are like drunk pigs in reverse. Noise levels and vibration can only be checked when the boat is on the move. And if it is an old boat on a wide canal, don't forget to check the width, as boats get wider around the middle with increasing years, much like people!

The haggling process must involve a survey of the boat by a qualified surveyor, who will find hundreds of ghastly faults which you can use to batter the price down. He may

Old wrecks can come very cheap.

Some secondhand boats need more attention than others!

also find a serious fault which will warn you that the boat is either dangerous or a complete bag of bolts fit only for the scrapyard. Normally you will want to look at boats that have the Certificate of Compliance, but as with new boats, this only covers the safety aspects of the craft; it doesn't guarantee that things like the water pumps or tanks are fit for use. Boats certified between 1990 and 1992 have had to pass fairly strict rules regarding the condition of the hull.

If you are a keen DIY enthusiast it is quite feasible to buy a complete wreck, either a burnt-out shell or a sunken hulk, and restore it. These boats tend to be so cheap that the expense of a survey is hardly worthwhile – you already know the boat is a wreck requiring thousands of pounds worth of work – but do make sure the thing won't sink just *after* you've completed the work!

A secondhand boat could be a stolen one,

so you will need to see the owner's original receipt; with very old boats this may well have got lost, in which case check the insurance documents to see that they are in order – insurance companies are quick to spot stolen engine numbers. However, boats are unique things and hard to disguise; there are very few stolen narrow boats and so the risk of buying one is not high.

Virtually all secondhand boats are sold on an 'As seen' basis, in other words if the thing blows up a week after you've bought it, that's your problem. It is therefore absolutely vital that you have the survey done *before* parting with any money. Boats that are on sale with brokers tend to have slightly better legal protection, since the broker will only transfer the funds to the vendor after a couple of weeks; if the boat turns out to be seriously different to the description given by the vendor, there is a chance of rectifying the matter. In a private sale, once the vendor has your cash it will normally take a court case to rectify any sharp practice.

It is important to obtain a bill of sale for a boat when you buy it secondhand, as well as a receipt: it needs to describe the boat and give its registration numbers, the serial number of the engine, and any other distinguishing features; it should also detail the vendor and buyer. The receipt needs to show the vendor, the buyer, the sum paid, and the boat. If there are any guarantees provided by the vendor these will need to be put in writing, though normally most transferred guarantees aren't worth the paper they're written on, so check if it's worth the bother.

There is one golden rule for secondhand boats: '*Caveat emptor*', which is Latin for *Buyer beware.*

Selling a Boat

The boot is on the other foot when it comes to selling your boat: you will be wanting to get the best price for it, usually so you can afford an even bigger one! If you are in any doubt as to the value of the craft a surveyor will be able to give you a valuation; this will cost about £10 or £20, and will give you a good base price to include in your advertisements in the canal magazines. A good advert describing the boat truthfully and in reasonable detail will undoubtedly attract the buyers; whereas if you say the boat is something which it is not, they will simply turn around and leave, and not only will you have broken the law but you will have wasted your own time as well as theirs.

Eventually someone will turn up who *does* want your boat. Take them for a cruise on it, which will convince them that it really is the wonderful specimen that you believe it to be! It is good practice to make up a book of all the boat's features, pumps, radios, engine manuals and suchlike; this will enable poten-

tial buyers to feel confident that they will be able to look after the boat once they've bought it. You should also provide all the documentation already described in 'Buying a Boat'.

There are plenty of people who will use this process to get a free day out on the canal at your expense, and there isn't much you can do about it. Furthermore, they might just be tempted into buying their own boat as a result, and it might even be yours! Complete novices can be irritating, particularly with questions like 'If they took out the locks the water would find its own level, wouldn't it?' What *do* they expect, a gentle slope down to the sea? Patience is a great virtue when it comes to selling boats.

Exceptional Transactions

It seems hard to believe, but there are still old boats lurking around the system which can be picked up for a song. In the Black Country there are sunken Joeys covered in weed just waiting for a fanatic to come along and restore them, and elsewhere other fine old wooden working boats lie abandoned and forgotten. It has to be a fanatic who wants them because the cost effectiveness of such a process simply does not make any kind of sense to a rational person. The transaction normally involves the purchaser taking the owner down to the pub and filling him with beer; the purchase price is often a whole pound, which is placed in the charity box on the bar.

This ensures the survival of boats that are simply not an economic proposition, but need to be saved so that our industrial heritage is preserved. If you own one of these boats you may find that the number of fanatics is almost as limited as the number of sunken historic boats, but don't despair, one will turn up one day. Surveyors and paperwork rarely figure in these transactions.

Still waiting for a fanatic . . .

Insurance

Any boat on the canal system should have a minimum of third party insurance. There are plenty of companies who will provide this, and usually boat policies are more comprehensive. It makes sense to cover all risks such as fire, theft, and damage from collision or sinking. Extra cover for tidal waters is essential if you intend to take the boat across river estuaries or any water affected by tides; this can be quite a long way inland on rivers like the Severn and the Trent.

The problem with insurance is that you can pay out a great deal of money each year and never know how good the policy or company is, until the dreaded day that you have to make a claim. It is only then that you discover that the small print excludes this or that, and you are left with a large bill. Insurance policies are not usually the most reader-friendly documents, and the day an insurance company gets an award from the Plain English Society will be a great day for boaters. You will have to read the document carefully, nevertheless.

Most insurers will not provide cover for boats over twenty years old unless they are provided with a recent surveyor's report stating that the hull and equipment are in good working order. Quite a few companies will not even consider providing cover for boats that do not have a Safety Certificate, and some have even restricted that to certificates issued on the basis of the first set of regulations rather than the more recent ones. The new Safety Certificate will have a section referring to hull integrity that can be completed by a qualified surveyor to let the insurers know that the boat is in good order.

Old boats never die.

Moorings

Moorings vary from luxurious marinas with showers, shops and bars, to the edge of a towpath at the back of an industrial estate full of vandals; the costs vary accordingly. British Waterways have a grading system that allows a set fee for a predetermined level of service. Private boat-yards are under no such obligation and tend to base their fees on the demand for their services. On the whole, private boatyards provide much more in the way of assistance to the boat owner, such as slipways, engine hoists, and many social aspects, all of which make their extra costs well worthwhile.

All boat-yards and marinas should be equipped with a certain level of fire safety equipment, and should include fire breaks between boats. A recent incident has brought the prospect of legislation in this particular

area a lot closer: one Cruiser was set on fire by vandals, and the fire spread along five boats before the emergency services could control the situation.

The Boat Safety Scheme

This is paperwork to drive boaters wild! The Certificate of Compliance was introduced in 1990 for private boats, and was based on ideas originally enforced in the 1980s for hire boats and residential craft. The underlying principles are that because the waterways contain confined spaces such as locks, efforts must be made to reduce the risks to other boats from accidents; and the general public, who frequently come to watch you drop your last windlass into the cut, also have to be protected from harm. British Waterways hoped that by working with the National Rivers

Authority and other bodies, a nationally recognized set of safety standards could be established; these could then be incorporated into the European Directive for Recreational Craft which was supposed to have been in place for the 1992 Single Market.

There probably isn't a single boat owner who isn't aware that things didn't quite work out as simply as this. Although British Waterways had a consultation period before the introduction of the 1990 'Grey Book', they were rather taken aback by the ferocity of complaints resulting from aggrieved boaters. It transpired that a large proportion of boats simply did not meet the specification and would be expensive to alter; moreover compliance for some boats was completely impossible, and their owners feared that they would lose a substantial asset. The regulations covering certain parts of the boats conflicted with the needs of river craft on waterways not controlled by British Waterways.

An amended version, the Boat Safety Scheme, was launched in 1993. This contains far less retrospective regulation so that older boats can carry on pottering along the cut until they are obsolete. British Waterways did a study to find out just how long boats lasted, to see whether they could omit old boats entirely from the scheme, and the results are marvellous for boaters, but not so good for the safety scheme. They discovered that if the new safety standards were implemented for all new boats, it would be ninety-eight years before all boats complied, and probably at least fifty before even half the boats could be considered safe; narrow boats last that long! The safety standards needed to be implemented in a much shorter time-span than their study suggested, and retrospective standards have had to be introduced.

The safety standards finally drawn up are considered to be the very minimum deemed necessary, and it doesn't reflect well on us

boaters that many consider these standards an unwarranted intrusion into our hobby, requiring extra expense. In truth, boats should really have met the standards long ago: there are reasons behind each one, and quite a few of those reasons are to be found in cemeteries. Moreover it is worth considering that what constitutes a minimum safety requirement, such as life buoys, may not be enough for your particular boat; it may be good enough to get the bit of paper, but will it be enough in the event of *your* boat capsizing?

The standards apply to virtually any boat bigger than a dinghy, and there follows a synopsis of the most important ones. The full standards are available from British Waterways; they will be sent to every licence holder and are likely to become obligatory in 1996. Part 1 refers to the scope of the scheme, the sorts of boats covered by it, and exemptions for maintenance craft. Unless you have a coastal boat using inland waterways for a transit crossing through Scotland, you will be expected to comply with all the others, although historic boats are allowed certain exemptions. Part 2 considers the most significant risks as identified by countless accidents. The clauses are set out below with a note to explain areas of confusion, or the motivation behind the rule.

2.1 *Filling pipes shall be taken to deck level or so arranged as to ensure that any fuel overflowing will not be discharged into any part of the vessel including the bilges.*

Simply put, this means that any spilt fuel has to run overboard; if it ran inboard it could become a fire risk. There are still plenty of petrol-powered boats around waiting for their chance to explode.

2.2 *The filling pipe shall have an internal diameter of at least 38mm (1½in), and any flexible hose shall be of non-kinking material suitable for the fuel used, and must be connected with leak-proof joints between the top* of the tank and a screw cap or plate forming the filling connection. All flexible hoses shall be adequately supported and of minimum practicable length, with all joints or connections readily accessible.

This one is common sense, since a kinked pipe or one too narrow will cause the fuel to airlock and splutter back out of the filler. The pipework has to be up to the job and easy to inspect; if it fails you could pump a lot of fuel into the bilges before you noticed something was wrong. Older boats with a 32mm (1¼in) filler pipe will be allowed to retain the original filler pipe.

2.3 All deck and fuel filling connections shall be situated so as to minimize the risk of cross-contamination and shall be clearly marked on the deck fittings or immediately beside them indicating the purpose of each connection and, in the case of fuel connections, the exact type of fuel.

A lot of people have complained that they don't want their boat cluttered up with little brass signs saying 'Diesel' or 'Water'; however, one chap was sitting on the toilet

Signs must be clearly visible.

smoking a cigarette when he discovered that some idiot had put twenty gallons of fuel into the waste-holding tank. This kind of confusion is bad for your health, and easy enough to prevent.

2.4 A vent pipe of minimum practicable length with an internal diameter of not less than 12mm (½in) shall be fitted at the highest point of every fuel tank and connected with leak-proof joints. The material used shall be non-kinking and approved for use with the fuel concerned.

A simple enough rule, to allow the vapour in a tank to escape. Existing boats can keep their 9mm (³/₈in) internal diameter vent pipe, and boats that have no vent at all are supposed to install a vent into the filler cap, provided that the vent has a flame arrester and minimum diameter of 12mm (½in). A vented filler cap will meet this specification.

2.5 A vent pipe shall extend to a height equal to, or greater than that of the deck filling connection, and the open end of a vent pipe shall be fitted in a position where no danger will be incurred from escaping fuel or vapour. Each opening shall be furnished with an effective wire-gauze-diaphragm flame arrester of non-corrosive material. The flame arrester shall be fitted with a gauze of mesh not less than 11 to the linear centimetre (28 to the linear inch), and the total area of the clear openings shall not be less than the cross-sectional area of the air pipe.

The clause is quite self-explanatory and easy to comply with. Fuel tanks must be vented, and they must be protected from nearby fires. The flame-arresting gauze is almost invariably fitted to every vent that you are likely to find in a chandlery.

2.6 Fuel tanks shall be properly secured, and be installed as low as practicable, and be constructed of a suitable non-corrosive material. Materials used in the construction of fuel tanks shall have a minimum fire resistance of 30 mins in accordance with BS476 part 20. Tanks shall have sustained a pressure test of

0.25 kgf/cm^2 (3.5 lbf/in^2) before installation, and be marked to indicate this. All joints and seams shall be efficiently welded, brazed or close-riveted to sustain a pressure test of 0.25 kgf/cm^2 (3.5 lbf/in^2.

Existing boats will not have to comply with the pressure test. However, if you replace a fuel tank it is a good idea to follow these specifications.

2.7 *No petrol or paraffin tank of more than 2.5 litres (½ gall) shall be installed within 1 metre (39½in) of any engine or heating appliance unless it is insulated and protected by an efficient baffle of fire-resistant material.*

Simple enough precaution to prevent the boat blowing up.

2.8 *Glass or plastic fuel sight gauges shall not be used. Fuel level indicators, if fitted, shall be of a type which does not allow escape of fuel or vapour in the event of damage to the indicator. Dipsticks when fitted shall be calibrated and only be used via gas-tight fittings. Where a dipstick is used it must be made so that it cannot strike the bottom of the tank.*

This clause should mean the end of the broomstick in the gas locker. Quite a few old tanks have had their bottoms worn out by repeated blows, since this is usually the only way that narrow boats have to check the fuel level. Old working boats will be allowed to keep their fuel systems, complete with historic glass sight gauges.

2.9 *Tanks shall be accessible and all connections shall be readily accessible for inspection.*

*Clause **2.8**: historic boats can keep their original engine installations.*

Hidden connections can lead to hidden fuel leaks, but it isn't easy to hide the fire caused by them.

2.10 *Tanks shall be effectively bonded by low-resistance metallic conductors of adequate strength to their deck filling connections, and in the case of a non-conducting deck or hull, tanks shall also be electrically bonded to an earth point in direct electrical contact with the surrounding water, for the discharge of static electricity.*

Almost all narrow boats are made of steel which is a good conductor of static. However, if you have a boat made of GRP the static electricity is a problem that has to be addressed. These standards also apply to other boats, which is why some of the clauses seem more appropriate to cruisers.

2.11 *Tanks may be drained only by means of a suitable drain valve fitted with a plug on the outlet.*

Most two-year-olds would take great delight in opening the valve and watching the fuel trickle into the bilges. They shouldn't be able to get past a screwed-on plug, though. This clause doesn't apply to existing boats that simply have a plug in the tank, but it isn't a bad idea to add a valve and plug when you get the chance (when the fuel tank is empty because you haven't been able to check the fuel level, perhaps).

2.12 *The fuel supply shall be drawn through the top of the tank, or as near to the top of the tank as is practicable, by means of an internal pipe extending to near the bottom of the tank. In the case only of gravity feed systems, a feed from a cock or valve directly screwed in near the bottom of the tank is permitted. Any return fuel line required to be connected to the fuel tank shall be connected through the top of the tank, or as near to the top of the tank as is practicable.*

This specification is designed to ensure that fuel systems will fail safe, and not dribble diesel into a fire, making matters worse.

2.13 *All fuel feeds and pipes permanently charged with fuel shall be made of softened copper, stainless steel, aluminium alloy or (for diesel installations only) mild steel of suitable size, fixed clear of exhaust systems and heating apparatus, and adequately supported to minimize vibration and strain. Any balance pipe between fuel tanks must comply with the requirements of this standard, and must in addition be fitted with valves directly attached to the tank and so constructed that they will not become slack when the valves are operated.*

The idea behind this one is to prevent fuel pipes suffering damage from corrosion or mechanical damage, since these represent one of the causes of engine-room fires.

2.14 *Flexible tubing may only be used in the engine compartment, and shall be suitable for the fuel used. It shall be of minimum practicable length, be reinforced, have an internal diameter of not more than half its external diameter, and have a fire-resisting quality as required by BS MA 102.*

The British Standard Fire Test referred to for this grade of fuel pipe has an international equivalent, ISO 7840. The hose is obtainable from most chandlers and quite a few diesel equipment stockists.

2.15 *All connections shall be made with efficient screwed, compression, cone, brazed or flanged joints. Soft-soldered joints shall not be used.*

Anyone who has tried to solder a joint that is good enough to hold diesel in will understand this. The oil will get through the most minute flaw, even a joint that is watertight under pressure may let diesel through. The solder gives way after repeated vibration as well.

2.16 *All fuel filters shall be suitable for marine use and shall be of fire-resistant quality.*

Cheap filters from a boot fair won't do: in the event of a fire they'll only make matters worse. Filters meeting the Fire Test Standard BS MA 102 or ISO 7840 should be fine.

2.17 *A cock or valve shall be fitted in the fuel feed pipe as near as possible to the fuel tank in a position where it is readily accessible. If it is not visible the position shall be clearly marked. In all petrol engine installations where the steering position is remote from the fuel tank, a second cock or means of operating the main cock or valve to close the tank shall be fitted immediately accessible from the steering position.*

This is an obvious safety measure, where the meaning of the words 'readily accessible' is crucial: if there is a fire on board you will need to be able to turn off the fuel supply very quickly, so 'readily accessible' means exactly that!

2.18 *Fuel pipes shall not be run in the bilge-water areas.*

If the bilges in your boat are anything like mine, you wouldn't want to see your worst enemy in there, let alone a fuel pipe!

2.19 *Carburettors (other than of the down-draught type) shall be fitted so as to allow any overflow therefrom to drain into a spirit-tight metal drip tray, the top of which shall be covered with copper or brass gauze of flame-arresting mesh soldered to the tray all round. The tray shall be removable or be fitted with a cock for emptying. A flame trap or air filter must be fitted to the air intake of petrol, petroil and paraffin engines.*

There aren't many petrol engines in narrow boats, and those that exist are a menace if not built to exacting standards. This clause is more applicable to river cruisers, but if you have a petrol engine in a narrow boat make sure it meets the above requirements, or better still save up for a diesel.

2.20 *The engine shall be securely installed.*

This clause may seem to be stating the obvious, but it is worth bearing in mind that 80 per cent of engine failures are caused by poor installation.

2.21 *Every vessel shall have an effective means of reversing, operable from the steering position. The engine stop control shall be located as near to the steering position as is practicable.*

It may be hard to believe that there are boats without a reverse gear, effectively meaning that they have no way of stopping, but there are some out there. Existing boats are exempt from this clause; one assumes they will become so battered by bumping into locks that they won't be around for very long! Interestingly enough, at the turn of the century when boat companies were first putting internal combustion engines into boats, an Irish fleet operator ordered a number of Bolinder engines without the complex reversing arrangement fitted; the suppliers queried this, since it was normal to have the reversing facility on a marine engine. They were told by the astute fleet operator that their horses didn't have a reverse gear, so why should they have one on an engine?

2.22 *An oil-tight tray made of metal or other suitable material, the sides of which must be carried up as high as practical, shall be fitted beneath every engine and gearbox so as to prevent leakage of oil escaping into any part of the vessel or overboard. A tray is not required if oil-tight structural members are fitted fore and aft of the engine. No fixed bilge pump is to draw from the oil-tight area.*

This is an anti-pollution measure inspired by the lumps of grease stuck to the ducks on the canals.

2.23 *The cylinders and exhaust system shall be effectively cooled and shall allow for the dissipation of heat. In the case of air-cooled engines or where water is not passed through the exhaust system, the exhaust pipe shall be effectively lagged or shielded.*

If you burned yourself whilst servicing the engine you'll know exactly what this means. The word 'effective' means that it must work properly, and not just look good: burns inflicted by silencers and exhaust pipes hurt!

2.4 *Exhaust noise shall be effectively suppressed, and no form of exhaust silencer cut-out shall be used.*

This is a clause that will re-appear in the European legislation for certain. Quite how our wonderful old vintage engines will comply with the regulations remains to be seen!

Clauses **2.25** and **2.26** refer to steam- and LPG-powered engine installations. If you have a steam or LPG engine in your boat it has to meet all sorts of regulations, and there just isn't room here to go into them all. The appropriate user group will be able to advise.

Part 3 of the Safety Scheme refers to the electrical installation. At present there are no standards governing the installation of 240-volt ac systems, so boaters still have plenty of opportunity to electrocute themselves unless they choose to follow the Code of Practice published by the British Marine Electronics Association. It is a good idea to follow it!

3.1 *All batteries shall be securely installed so as to prevent movement and damage. All battery compartments shall be adequately ventilated and covered with insulating and non-corrosive material. No battery may be fitted beneath or adjacent to any petrol or LPG tank, cylinder, cock, pipe or filter.*

I once set foot on a boat, and immediately leapt off again at speed having seen a metal petrol can stored on top of the battery; the only thing that was stopping the battery short-circuiting through the petrol can was a layer of flaking paint, and if it *had* shorted the can would have exploded as effectively as any bomb. There can be a lot of power stored in a battery, and it needs to be treated with respect!

3.2 *Cables shall be of adequate current-carrying capacity and of suitable construction and grade. They shall be insulated and/or sheathed so as to be impervious to attack by fuel or water. They shall be adequately supported, or run in adequately supported suitable conduit.*

This clause effectively rules out boats wired with bits of old bell wire. There are quite a few out there.

3.3 *Main circuits shall be installed above bilge water level, and all except starter circuits shall be protected by circuit breakers or fuses of the appropriate rating and of a suitable design.*

A simple enough requirement.

3.4 *All cables shall be installed as high as is practicable in the vessel, and they shall be run clear of all sources of heat such as exhaust pipes. They shall not be run adjacent to fuel or gas pipes unless contained in suitable conduit. PVC insulated and/or sheathed cables shall not be run in direct contact with polystyrene insulation.*

House builders have known for some years that polystyrene insulation damages PVC, and the combination has been forbidden for a long time. Boats that have this problem will not need to instantly rip out all their cabin linings, but the electrical system will need to be tested for electrical insulation breakdown at regular intervals; when the test shows a problem developing, then the wiring circuit will need to be replaced. Wire shouldn't be run next to chimneys and flues from water heaters, as these can be just as damaging as an exhaust pipe.

3.5 *A master battery switch capable of disconnecting the system (including the starter circuits) shall be installed in a readily accessible position as close to the battery as possible. The battery master switch must be capable of carrying the maximum current of the system. Electric bilge pumps, security alarms and fire pumps when fitted may have circuits which bypass the master switch, but only if separately protected by fuses.*

You'll probably want this switch when the insulation breaks down on the wire next to the polystyrene and starts an electrical fire. The switch will need a rating of at least 150 amps to cope with the engine starter motor. It is a good policy to switch if off when the boat is unattended.

3.6 *Main starter motor leads subject to high current shall have soldered or pressure-crimped connectors. Spark plug leads shall be supported clear of the engine block and cylinder head.*

Quite apart from the safety aspect, this clause will ensure much more trouble-free engine operation. Dodgy connections and chafing high-tension leads are a major cause of breakdowns.

3.7 *All electrical devices fitted in any compartment containing petrol or gas shall be ignition-protected in accordance with BS 7489.*

This is now BSEN 28846, but it says the same thing. Sparks from switches and motors can ignite fuel vapour, but ignition-protected equipment prevents this from happening.

3.8 *All electrical equipment shall be two-wire insulated, except in respect of the engine circuits where there must be a low-resistance return conductor between the battery and the engine. Engine installations with two-wire insulated electrical systems do not require fitting of the low-resistance return conductor.*

This clause specifies that the hull should not be used as any part of the electrical system (as detailed in Chapter 3); all electrical equipment must have a positive from the battery and a negative return to it.

3.9 *The spark ignition and generating systems of engines and all electrical equipment on the vessel shall be effectively suppressed against causing radio and television interference.*

This requirement really applies to any electrical equipment on boats or elsewhere. It can be a problem stopping those little fluorescent lights whining away on AM radio, but the problem needs to be solved. Some petrol engines can cause dreadful interference.

Part 4 of the Boat Safety Scheme relates to electrically-propelled boats, and since only very few narrow boats have electric power plants, the space available doesn't justify a detailed examination of this section. In years to come electric boats will become more popular, much as they were at the turn of the century. New specifications for charging points are being drawn up, and one day someone will invent a better battery which will make the idea much more feasible.

Part 5 relates to outboard and portable engines. There are very few narrow boats powered by outboards, apart from the small 'Cub'-type boats. However, there are plenty of boats carrying portable generators, although these can represent a serious fire risk since they are usually petrol engines.

5.1 and **5.2** in effect duplicate Part 2 relating to fuel pipes, deck fittings and so on.

5.3 *Portable fuel tanks carried inboard and connected by flexible piping to the engine carburettor, and close-coupled fuel tanks forming an integral part of the engine, may be used providing that the fuel supply can be readily shut off, and that no unauthorised modifications are made to the equipment as supplied by the manufacturers. Portable fuel tanks shall be clearly marked with the type of fuel to be used, and when not in use shall be stowed in accordance with standards **7.2** and **7.3**.*

This standard hopes to eliminate Heath Robinson-type jury-rigged tanks which have not been tested by the manufacturer. Petrol spillages from home-made fuel tanks are a major cause of boat fires. The standards **7.2** and **7.3** normally relate to gas installations, but petrol vapour behaves in a very similar manner and needs to be vented overboard to avoid the risk of explosion.

5.4 *Petrol not carried in fuel tanks shall be stowed in containers conforming with the requirements of the Petroleum Spirit (Motor Vehicles, &c) Regulations 1929 (SR & 0 1929/952) or the Petroleum Spirit (Plastic Containers) regulations S.I. 1982 No 630, and these shall be stowed in accordance with standard **7.2** and **7.3**.*

This sounds a mouthful, but in essence it means that you must store petrol in containers manufactured for the purpose, and these must be stored in a locker ventilated in the same way as required for gas.

5.5 relates to engines powered by LPG, and as far as I know there aren't any narrow boats of this design. If you have one, it must meet the LPGITA Code of Practice No 18.

5.6 to **5.8** effectively duplicate other standards. **5.8** again stresses the importance of storing LPG and engines and fuel tanks in lockers which will vent gas and fuel vapour overboard. Furthermore, you must never store petrol and gas in the same locker: several people have been terribly burnt and some even killed by explosions and fires caused by petrol containers brought into a boat. It might sound like a nuisance to store them in a separate locker outside, but it really is a life-saving regulation.

Part 6 concerns fire prevention and extinguishing equipment, and it shouldn't be a surprise that these are in the standards – narrow boats have so many ways of catching fire that it is important to be able to attempt to extinguish a fire before it catches hold. However, once a fire has a grip on the boat there is only one option available: to get out. If under way, steer to the bank, get all the people off the boat, and turn off the fuel and gas stop taps immediately. If possible, use the fire extinguishers to combat the fire, but if there is the slightest danger to yourself from smoke or heat, get out of the cabin. If the gas locker is away from the area of the fire, disconnect the cylinders and get them off the boat, otherwise get yourself off. The insurance policy should be able to sort out a new boat, so concentrate on saving your family and yourself.

6.1 *Powered vessels or vessels carrying or fitted with cooking, heating, refrigerating or lighting appliances shall be equipped with not less than the number of portable extinguishers detailed below, which shall be of a type approved by the BSI and/or British Approvals of Fire Equipment scheme. Extinguishers shall be kept in readily accessible positions adjacent to fire-risk points, and shall be properly maintained in good condition for immediate use. Any portable extinguisher provided for the protection of an engine space shall be capable of being discharged without fully opening the primary access.*

Length of vessel	Minimum number of extinguishers	Minimum fire rating of each extinguisher	Minimum combined fire rating of extinguishers
up to 7m	2	5A/34B	10A/68B
7m – 11m	2	5A/34B	13A/89B
over 11m	3	5A/34B	21A/144B

The number of extinguishers may be reduced by one with a fire rating of no more than 5A/34B where either (a) no cooking, heating, refrigeration, lighting or fuel burning appliances are carried; or (b) no engine is installed.

This is the comprehensive clause specifying what extinguishers must be on board: narrow boats are powered vessels, even if your engine is in bits on the kitchen table. The fire-risk points on the boat are the galley and engine room, although if you are a smoker you can add the bedroom and lounge as well. In effect it means that wherever you are on the boat, a fire extinguisher should be no more than two paces away from you. The part relating to opening the primary access of an engine space is particularly relevant to Cruiser-style narrow boats, because if there is a fire under the stern deck you will want to be able to discharge an extinguisher into the space through a small hole – if you lift one of the main deck-boards, the flames will shoot up at your face.

Fire-fighting equipment must be accessible.

Fire extinguishers used to be measured by the weight of the gas or powder; now they are measured by their ability to fight fires, and their rating is marked on them. In the event of a fire you will discover that they discharge very quickly, and to get the best effect it is important to use them accurately on the base of the fire. In fact it does no harm to double the number set out by the regulations; it is a *minimum* standard, not a recommendation.

6.2 *Any fixed system installed for the protection of a fire-risk space shall be in addition to the portable extinguishers required by standard* **6.1** *and if remotely operated, the release device shall be readily accessible from outside that space.*

This refers to automatic extinguisher systems inside engine compartments; they are mostly fitted to larger cruisers, although some narrow boats have them. They are usually halon-type extinguishers which can be retained until their life-expiry date. Halon extinguishers are very good at putting out fires, though unfortunately it is alleged that they can seriously damage the ozone layer.

6.3 *In vessels fitted with cooking facilities, a fire blanket marked as complying with the 'light duty' requirements of BS 6575 and ready for immediate use, shall be kept nearby.*

Simple enough to comply with this rule, though I wonder how many boat owners' houses have one?

6.4 *In vessels with hulls constructed of glass-fibre-reinforced plastic (GRP) those areas of high fire risk, such as an engine room or fuel compartment, shall have any exposed GRP structure coated with suitable fire-retardant material complying with the Class 2 requirements of BS 476: Part 7.*

This clause does not apply to many narrow boats since most are made of steel; there is also an exemption for boats registered prior to the introduction of the scheme. However, there are a number of boats with GRP superstructures which even though they are not obliged to comply with this standard, would be well advised to do so for their own safety.

6.5 *Polystyrene thermal insulation shall comply with the Type A requirements of BS 3837: Part 1.*

Boats which are already registered and fitted with insulation that doesn't comply with this requirement are exempt, but when the boat is refitted it makes sense to use fire-retardant insulation, or a completely inert insulating material like fibreglass or rockwool.

6.6 *All soft furnishing, fabrics and foam materials used in the lining out and furnishing of vessels shall be of suitable fire-resistant materials, which on combustion release minimal amounts of toxic products. Upholstery fabrics used shall satisfy the cigarette and butane flame tests of BS 5852: Part 1.*

Again, existing boats are exempt from this requirement, although it is certainly worth complying with.

6.7 *All vessels shall have two means of escape from accommodation areas. All means of escape shall have a minimum clear opening of 0.2m² (310in²) and a minimum width of 380mm (15in).*

Private boats made before 1 August 1993 are not required to comply with this standard where it is not practical to modify the structure to provide two means of escape. However, this won't be a lot of comfort in the event of a fire. To illustrate the fact that these are minimum standards, try making a cardboard frame containing an aperture of the size specified, and decide whether you could use it as an escape hatch; it really is a very small hole. A window can provide a second means of escape if it can be either opened or broken

out, and as long as it is big enough; a fixed window would have to be broken in order to be an escape route, so a hammer to break it must be attached in a clearly visible position beside it. Special windscreen-breaking hammers are available cheaply enough from most motorist shops.

Part 7 deals with LPG (Liquified Petroleum Gas) installations and is one of the most comprehensive and specific parts of the Boat Safety Scheme; unlike other sections, very few of the standards have been relaxed after the first edition was reviewed. The reasons are simple; LPG installations are the single biggest cause of serious incidents, and pose the greatest danger to boats and their crews. Since virtually all narrow boats rely on LPG for cooking and frequently refrigeration and heating too, these standards have a particular relevance. Their implementation may require some alterations to be carried out on some boats, and this needs to be carried out by a qualified person.

7.1 *The installation shall comply with BS 5482 'Domestic Butane and Propane Gas Burning Installations, Part 3: Installations in Boats, Yachts and other Vessels' except that: (a) the pressure drop of 2.5 mbar specified in Appendix C may be exceeded if, when all burners are lit, the flames are steady and of the correct proportions; (b) open flue spillage tests as required by Clause 4.3.2 of BS 5440 Part 1 need not be conducted if the ventilation arrangements fully comply with the requirements of BS 5482 Part 3; (c) the pipe sizes recommended in BS 5482 Part 3 are to be regarded as for guidance only.*

This clause highlights what has to be one of the biggest mistakes the narrow boat building industry has ever made. The British Standard referred to has always applied to narrow boats, and it has been in effect since 1956; thousands of boats have been built

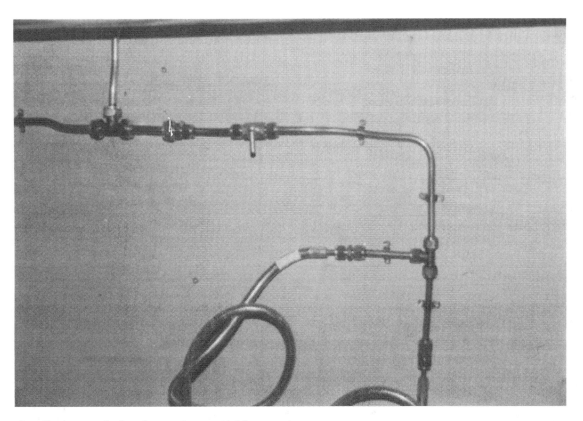

A well-supported, clear layout is essential for gas pipes.

since then, that don't merely ignore the requirements of the standard, but could be positively lethal.

7.2 *Every container (whether in use or not) shall be either: (i) secured on an open deck away from hatches and other openings so that any escaping gas is dispersed overboard; or (ii) secured in a separate compartment or box above the water-line, with gas-proof and flame-retarding sides and bottom, and with a lid or cover. Such a compartment or box shall be of sufficient depth to contain the height of the cylinder(s), cylinder valve(s), and regulator(s). Such a compartment or box shall have provision for allowing any escaping gas to be vented overboard by means of a metal or flexible pipe suitable for use with LPG, or a direct opening through the side of the vessel as near*

as is practicable to the bottom of the compartment or box. The lower pipe or opening shall have a minimum internal diameter of 12mm (½in) for a cylinder of up to 15kg capacity, and shall be enlarged in cross-sectional area proportionately for additional gas storage.

At least most boat builders can make gas lockers! Though some of them do put the vents below the water-line, which means they cannot work. Storing gas bottles on an open deck avoids the need to fabricate a gas locker on an old boat, but it does leave the bottle vulnerable to theft.

7.3 *Any compartment or box as specified under standard 7.2 (ii) shall be constructed of sheet metal of 0.9mm (20 w.g.) minimum thickness with joints welded or brazed, or of* *fire-retarding glassfibre-reinforced plastic of adequate thickness. The materials used in the construction of a locker or compartment shall have a fire resistance of 30 min in accordance with BS 476 Part 20.*

There is rarely a problem for narrow boats with this standard, since boat builders usually use the same sheet thickness for the gas locker as the superstructure, and exceed the minimum by several millimetres.

7.4 *All containers shall be installed in an upright position with the valve uppermost, and not adjacent to any cooking or heating appliance, or in an engine or fuel or battery compartment.*

This standard is to protect gas bottles from damage from other sources; its meaning also includes what should be considered as a total ban on keeping the petrol can for your generator in the same gas locker as the gas bottle. If you are storing petrol cans on a boat they will need their own vented locker. Quite what would happen to a gas locker containing both petrol and gas in the event of a fire I'm not sure, but no doubt it would be pretty spectacular!

7.5 *Ready access to the main gas valve(s) shall be provided at all times. If the main gas valve(s) are not visible, their position(s) shall be clearly marked.*

In all the standards, 'clearly marked' means that a stranger on the boat, for instance a fireman, can quickly see and read the label – a small, tarnished brass plate won't be good enough in an emergency.

7.6 *Pressure regulators may be mounted either separately from the cylinder(s) or with a direct connection to the cylinder(s). Pressure regulators not direct-connected to cylinders shall be securely fixed and suitably protected within the compartment specified in standard **7.2** (ii). In both cases a flexible connection to BS 3212 Type 2 shall be fitted to facilitate the replacement of cylinders. Pressure regulators of the external manual-adjustment type shall not be fitted.*

This standard is designed to ensure that the correct regulator is used, and that any automatic change-over valves are correctly mounted. It is also important to ensure that your regulator is capable of allowing the required volume of gas to pass through it. Some small regulators cannot pass enough gas through them to allow high power appliances like certain water heaters to function correctly. A pressure drop will result from this.

7.7 *Each point intended for use with a portable appliance shall be provided with a readily accessible control tap, and a bayonet or screwed connection.*

Simple enough.

7.8 *Where self-contained portable gas appliances are used, with the burner screwed direct to the container, such appliances if stored in the vessel shall be placed in a compartment or locker constructed in accordance with standard **7.2** (ii). Self-contained portable gas appliances shall not be used whilst unattended on board any vessel.*

This refers to those little camping stoves, and other similar devices; they have to be stored in the gas locker. And although it might not appear to apply to narrow boats, plenty of people keep a propane or butane blow-torch on board, and this should also be kept in the proper locker.

7.9 *Flexible tubing conforming to BS 3212 Type 2 of minimum practicable length and fitted with integral threaded metallic ends shall be used, (i) for the immediate connections to containers, or to regulators directly attached thereto but not extended to the interior of the vessel or outside a vented container housing; and (ii) for the connections between portable appliances and their control points.*

All Calor gas stockists will be able to supply tubing to this specification; bits of old plastic pipe tend to rupture under pressure and waste the gas. This pipe is usually date-stamped, so you will be able to see how old it is. The 'integral threaded metallic ends' phrase is being deleted from future editions of the Safety Scheme.

7.10 *All fixed pipework other than that which forms an integral part of gas-burning appliances shall be made of solid drawn copper or stainless steel.*

I know we have far less stringent rules about domestic gas pipes, but houses don't get banged into locks that regularly. In much the same way that the electrical wire on board needs to be suitable for a vessel, so do the gas pipes.

7.11 *All fixed pipework shall be as short, and run as high as practicable, and shall be rigidly secured. It shall be adequately protected against mechanical damage and deterioriation.*

The simplest way to achieve this is to have a duct along the corner of the ceiling, on the opposite side of the boat to the electrical duct; a pipe run along the inside of the gunwale is usually considered all right. The pipes shouldn't be routed anywhere where they can be hit.

7.12 *No pipework shall be run through the bilge-water area, or adjacent to electric cables (unless the cables are contained in suitable conduit, see standard 3.4), or adjacent to exhaust pipes, or in any other position prejudicial to its safety.*

It shall not be run through petrol engine compartments, and/or compartments specifically designed to contain or containing electrical equipment including batteries, unless carried in gas-proof conduit admitting jointless pipe only.

Something of a mouthful, this standard! It is self-explanatory though, and ensures the gas pipe won't be damaged by short-circuits, burning or corrosion.

7.13 *Joints in pipework shall be kept to a minimum, and they shall be readily accessible for inspection. Joints shall be made with compression fittings and rigidly secured. (Note: when gas is not being used, it is advis-*

able to turn off the valve on the container.) Where two containers are connected to a manifold or tee, both container valves should be closed before either container is disconnected. Any spare or empty containers on board must either be on deck or in the ventilated housing,

The main places where gas systems develop leaks are in the joints; these also reduce the flow of gas and increase the pressure drop when the system is being used. Smooth curves in the pipes allow the gas to flow that much more easily along its length. Compression fittings are essential; it isn't a very good idea to take a blow-lamp onto a soldered joint when there is propane behind it!

7.14 *An approved gas test point shall be fitted at the furthest practicable point from the supply. (Note: an approved bubble tester is highly recommended in order that boat owners may check easily for gas leaks. Such a tester shall be securely fixed in the gas-tight compartment or box as defined by standards* **7.2** *and* **7.3**.*)*

The gas test point can be fitted by a Calor gas or CORGI registered fitter, and various firms make a selection of bubble testers, in particular for cookers and fridges on boats. It is also possible to get a pressure gauge which fits between the regulator and cylinder, and which will indicate any leaks. Since minor leaks are hard to detect simply by smelling for gas, these testers can provide valuable early warning of a problem.

Part 8 is concerned with appliances, and deals with things like cookers and heaters, fridges and lighting. A lot of these appliances will have continuously burning pilot lights which are easy to forget about. If you have a petrol engine, or even a petrol generator, do remember to turn off all these pilot lights before filling the fuel tank. Put those cigarettes out, too!

8.1 *All fuel installations for cooking, heating,*

refrigerating and lighting appliances shall be installed in accordance with the appropriate parts of these standards.

This has to be the ultimate catch-all clause: if you have a gas-fired cooker, the gas standards apply, if it is a diesel unit then the diesel fuel standards apply; electric lights have to meet the electrical standards. Something of a duplication, really.

8.2 *The pilot lights and/or burners on all gas or paraffin refrigerators installed in petrol-engined vessels shall be completed enclosed. Air for combustion must be (i) drawn and exhausted through an approved flame trap; or (ii) piped to the appliance from outside the vessel, or from a point inside the vessel above the level of the ports, windows or other means of ventilation in the compartment in which the appliance is installed.*

A clause to gladden the heart of everyone with a diesel engine!

8.3 *All LPG or fuel oil appliances of the catalytic type, or with pilot lights, or having continuously burning flames, shall incorporate a flame failure device to cut off the gas or fuel supply to the main and pilot burners. Catalytic appliances shall also comply in all respects with the requirements of BS 5258 Part 11.*

It is probably impossible to buy appliances without flame failure devices fitted nowadays. Some old equipment may be rendered obsolete by this standard, but there's a good chance that it will be very old and due for the scrap heap anyway.

8.4 *Appliances fired by fuel oil shall have a valve or cock to shut off the supply in a readily accessible position within the same compartment as, but at a safe distance from, the appliances.*

This clause is to ensure that should your diesel-fired heater, or whatever, burst into flames, you can turn it off. The tap will need to be a couple of feet away from the unit so that it can be operated without having to plunge your hand through the fire to reach it.

8.5 *Woodwork and all other combustible materials, including curtains adjacent to all appliances, shall be suitably insulated and protected against excessive heat, or be inherently flame-retardant, or be treated with a durable flame retardant.*

This standard is a partial duplication of standard **6.6**, but with great emphasis on the effect of the appliances.

8.6 *All permanently installed domestic cooking, heating, lighting or refrigerating appliances shall be secured in order to eliminate undue strain on pipework or fittings, and to prevent overturning in the event of a collision, and they shall be properly installed.*

This is designed to prevent you being chased around the cabin by your cooker after you've banged into a lock. The last phrase 'and shall be properly installed' means that the installation *must* comply with the manufacturers' instructions.

8.7 *Oil-fired or LPG appliances shall not be installed in the engine space in petrol-engined vessels.*

8.8 *Every fuel-burning appliance which requires a flue and, where fitted, a draught diverter, shall be of an approved type and properly fitted and maintained. The flue shall be of adequate internal diameter, effectively insulated, and of suitable material to ensure safe passage of gases to the outside of the vessel.*

Boat builders are still ignoring this standard, and some surveyors seem happy to let them do so. Water heaters are supplied with a flue of a certain length by the manufacturer, and the flue shouldn't be shortened. People do it though, and it then poses a risk to the safety of the people on board. Solid fuel stoves need to have the correct flue fitted, too, although in their case the exhaust gases are so acrid they make everyone abandon ship. LPG exhaust gases simply suffocate people in their sleep – a nice gentle way to go, but not yet if you don't mind, boat builders!

8.9 *The water inlet to any water heater shall be piped only from the vessel's cold water system.*

This clause might seem spurious, but it is there to stop people taking the feed to a water heater from a source of already hot water. Most gas water heaters don't have thermostats, and so if the water going into them is at 80° C (as heated in a calorifier), they will then happily add another 30° and blast the poor person in the shower with super-heated steam.

8.10 *Adequate ventilation of a type which cannot be shut off shall be provided in accordance with the requirements of BS 5482 Part 3 in vessels in which LPG or liquid fuel appliances are used. (Note: ventilators should be weathertight to cater for the worst conditions likely to be encountered by the vessel.)*

We have already discussed the importance of good ventilation. The note about weathertight ventilators applies to yachts on the waterways, since theirs need to keep out the water when they are in an Atlantic storm; narrow boats aren't expected to encounter such conditions.

Part 9 concerns pollution:
No sanitation system capable of discharging sewage overboard shall be fitted in any vessel unless it is capable of being sealed or rendered inoperable. Sanitation systems shall comply with the requirements of BS MA 101.

This standard is clear enough, although existing boats will not be expected to meet the BS MA 101 part.

Part 10 applies to new and hire boats so doesn't concern us here; and the exemptions in Part 11 have been incorporated into the notes.

Annex A: this has been a political hot potato and a real thorn in the sides of the people trying to bring all the different authorities' standards into harmony: as a result, it barely exists in the Boat Safety Scheme. If you have a copy of the original 1990 Boat Standards you can bring your boat into accordance with that and be reasonably certain that it is meeting the basic minimum safety requirements for the construction and equipments. This is not always possible, hence the uproar when the standards were introduced. It is no longer compulsory to meet these original standards but if you adhere to as many of them as possible, you can't go too far wrong.

It has been hard work itemizing this list of standards, and I hope you have managed to persevere this far! The standards are there to reduce the risk of avoidable accidents and not, as some people seem to believe, to make boaters' lives more difficult. But in spite of our marathon journey, one unpleasant fact remains: that far more people are injured on the waterways because they get between the boat and a bridge or lock, than are ever hurt because of a structural fault in the boat. The standards are silent on this, and most boaters would wish it to stay this way: driving tests would be anathema to the free spirits on the water. However, to keep the casual atmosphere of canals intact, it is up to all of us to be careful when we're driving our boats. And although this section on boat safety seems to be full of dire warnings about hideously life-threatening accidents just waiting to happen, the reality is that boating is a very safe leisure activity.

— 8 —

Cruising Skills and Equipment

It might seem odd to leave the real cruising part until last, but then the boat does need to be in good order before it sets off. Most boats tend to be maintained 'on the hoof'; after all, whilst the boat is tied up the systems on board aren't usually working, and it's only

Traditional boats need lots of polishing!

when you're exploring those interesting nooks and crannies of the canal system that the boat and its equipment is expected to work at full load. This is when a poorly maintained boat will start to go wrong, and when Murphy's Law – the principle of the sheer cussedness of the universe – comes into action. Thus, boats never run out of coal by a coalyard, but on some windswept hillside miles from anywhere; and the propeller will wait until you are cruising past a weir on a fast-flowing river before it bites into an old mattress. Nevertheless, long cruises exploring new waterways are great fun, though a good boat is an essential prerequisite for a good holiday.

Life-saving Equipment

Before you set off, make sure that both you and your boat have taken on board adequate life-saving skills and equipment. First, learn to swim. The old boatmen never learnt to swim, which resulted in many of them drowning. It's no good saying 'Well, I've just spent twenty thousand pounds on a boat and I'm damned if I'll go swimming after that!' because if you fall off the boat you'll need to. Swimming is good exercise, and can save your life; boating is all about water, and *every* boater needs to be able to swim, and preferably to save a non-swimmer from danger.

Canals are usually shallow and muddy, and falling into them is dangerous because the mud can trap a person's legs. Canals and rivers are also very cold, and it only takes a few minutes for the cold to weaken the strongest swimmer; if someone does slip off the boat it is therefore vital to rescue them quickly. Stop the boat and deploy the lifebuoy. Never reverse the boat towards someone in the water because the wash of the propeller can drag them into it – if there is room, turn the boat so that the bows are closest to the person overboard. If you are in the water the sides of a boat look very high and are quite bare of hand grips; it is an unpleasant place to be!

Lifebuoys

The safety standards require a minimum of one lifebuoy to be accessible to the steerer, but it doesn't hurt to have more on board, even though they do take up a lot of space. They will need to be inspected regularly to ensure they are still in good condition: the rope handles must not be frayed, and the plastic structure shouldn't be broken.

If you have to throw the lifebuoy to someone in the water, *don't* aim for his head because if the buoy hits him it can knock him out; try to get it to land just in front of him. A bit of practice is worthwhile. There are also throwable floating lifelines available these days, which are less likely to knock the victim unconscious, and take up much less space on board. However, they should not be regarded as a substitute for the old-fashioned life-ring.

Lifebuoys must be within reach of the steerer.

Buoyancy Aids

'Life-jackets' are essential for non-swimmers and children, and are available in a selection of grades and sizes. For inland waterways you won't need the heavy duty ones designed for the North Sea, but you will need ones that have the correct buoyancy for the weight of the wearer. Most buoyancy aids have a complicated set of ties and straps to prevent the person slipping out of them, and it is important to keep these clean and untangled. When putting them on, ensure that they are correctly fitted. As the boat owner, it is your responsibility to make sure that a holiday doesn't end in tragedy.

Tools for Basic Maintenance

Tool-Box

Even the most perfectly maintained boat is likely to need a bit of attention, and a comprehensive tool-box will enable any repairs to be carried out efficiently. A full set of ring spanners to suit the engine are essential, plus an adjustable spanner, which might not be good for the nuts and bolts, but there's bound to be one nut that won't fit any of the spanners on board.

A reasonably comprehensive screwdriver kit is also essential. A 12in (30cm) hacksaw and heavy duty wire cutters are useful for removing tyres and mattresses from the propeller, a Stanley knife is good for polythene bags. A 30in (76cm) bow-saw is a bulky item, but it can be invaluable for clearing branches of fallen trees, as well as cutting up logs for the stove. The boat should have a big hammer for driving mooring stakes, and for threatening a reluctant engine.

Spare Parts

A supply of consumable items like fuses, jubilee clips, spare fuel hose and silicon sealant are worth bringing on board, and the engine will require a whole stock of its own spare parts: fan belt, water hoses, water pump, gasket kit and fuel filter are all essential. If you are an enthusiastic engineer you'll be able to think of your own list of components liable to failure. The cabin equipment shouldn't normally need any attention during a cruise, but it is worth keeping a spares kit for the drinking-water pump, since its breakdown can have such an adverse effect on the holiday.

Essential Cruising Equipment

Windlasses

A collection of windlasses to match all the various paddle gear you are likely to encounter is vital. Windlasses are gradually becoming standardized, but you will find that the process hasn't got that far. The normal twin-socket windlass will deal with most sorts, and the old-fashioned small-sized 'Oxford' windlass, although obsolete, fits worn spindles far better than new equipment.

As the population of boaters is getting older, so the effort required to raise some paddles seems greater. It is possible to buy geared windlasses, which make life easier; these come on and off the market at regular intervals – I suspect that the market is too small to sustain a regular manufacturer. If you need one and no one seems to be currently selling them, they can be made up by an engineer. The socket is welded to an epicyclic reduction gear, often called a 'torque doubler', and you will need to take the engineer for a boat trip so he can see what you're talking about.

There are parts of the system where you'll need specialist equipment or keys to operate the locks. A hefty piece of 2 x 3in (5 x 7cm) oak will come in handy on some canals.

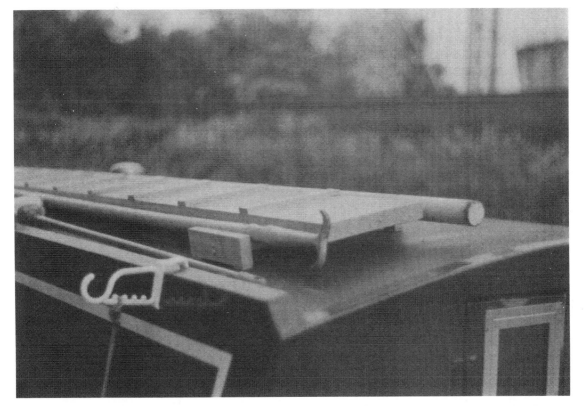

Poles, hooks and planks need an annual inspection.

Gangplanks, Poles and Hooks

That collection of wood on the roof has a function. There are boat poles, which will need to be examined at the start of each season to check that they haven't become cracked or rotten. Boat poles are designed to push the boat gently into position. They are not levers and will break if used as such, nor are they suitable for fending off rogue boats, either; a pole can turn into a spear if it breaks, and you don't want to be in front of it when this happens. Treat them carefully. Poles usually come in two sizes, a ten foot (3m) one for pushing the bows and stern into position, and a five foot (1.5m) one for tunnel work.

Years ago the old boatmen used to use the five-footer to prop up lift bridges when they were cruising alone; the Oxford canal has more than its fair share of these, and the old working boats used to lift the bridge and prop it up with the pole. The boat would then cruise through and once he was clear, the helmsman would pull the pole out with a rope he had tied to it; the bridge then descended with a crash. This sort of boating technique resulted in many bridges collapsing and being replaced with higher fixed ones, no doubt to the boatmen's great delight. Naturally no one could possibly recommend this practice today: it is fraught with dangers and hazards. It is worth knowing, though.

The gangplank has a dual function. As the canals get shallower, the gap between the moored boat and the bank gets bigger and the plank is needed to span this gap, which it should do easily. The plank must be up to the job – a thin piece of plywood is going to break, so be sure that what you have is sufficiently substantial; scaffolding planks are a favourite. An annual inspection, and treatment with wood preservative are essential.

The gang plank's secondary purpose is to prop open bottom gates that won't open wide enough. The traditional length of the plank is seven feet (2.1m), which means the plank can be placed between the two bottom gates, or single gate and the wall, and hold them apart; the boat can then cruise out of the lock, under the plank. This trick is usually only needed in the spring when there is an accumulation of winter debris behind the gates preventing them from opening fully. If the gates are still impossible to open, you'll have to fish around behind them with the boat hook to dislodge the obstruction.

The boat hook is an invaluable tool. A good quality galvanized steel hook on an eight foot (2.4m) pole will come in handy for all sorts of tasks, from pulling the boat into the side, to retrieving items blown off the boat by the wind. They need the same care in use as a pole.

Ropes

Ropes are essential. The boat will have quite a selection of bits of string hanging from it already, and a basic rope kit which consists of a pair of thirty foot (9m) long lines, fore and aft, a pair of shorter ones for tying up, and a centre line for lock work. The ropes can be made of polypropylene, hemp, nylon or cotton, as long as they are strong enough for the job. Naturally a dirty bit of blue polypropylene is going to look incongruous on a fine traditional Josher, but the looks are secondary to its function; beautiful white laid cotton might look better, but if it is rotten inside it could cause an accident.

Each waterway and each boater have their own requirements from ropes, so it is difficult to suggest the best lengths. Whatever the type and length, it is important to make sure that the rope is unfrayed, and in the case of plant-derived ropes, not going rotten. Spare ropes are a useful reserve, since one night tied up to a rusty mooring ring can ruin a rope.

Fenders

Narrow boats have bow and stern fenders to prevent them crashing into lock gates and other boats too hard. The traditional fender is a complicated knot of rope, usually made out of old mooring lines tied around a cork core. These old hessian fenders will last a long time if they are given a treatment of creosote every few years; this involves removing the fender from the boat, and liberally soaking it with dark brown creosote. The fender will need to dry thoroughly before being replaced on the craft – no one wants a fine film of creosote polluting the canal.

Modern fenders are made just the same way, but out of brown polypropylene rope which won't rot and so doesn't need any treatment. They may get clogged up with mud, particularly the front one, and need a strong hosing down with fresh water. The stern fender has to prevent the back of the boat and the rudder from being damaged, and so needs to project beyond the rudder to achieve this. However, as stern fenders get older they tend to droop, and no longer reach to the end of the rudder; it helps to turn them upside-down once a year to even out the effect of gravity.

Fenders are not really given due credit for what they do: they are expected to slow down and stop a fifteen- or twenty-ton boat travelling at a couple of miles an hour, all in the space of four inches, and at the same time prevent any damage occurring to the boat or lock gate as well. This is asking a lot. If the fender falls off and you bump into a lock gate, you will realize just how valuable they are. Good fenders will save a fortune in broken plates!

Fenders need to reach beyond the rudder.

Fender supports need a strut beneath them to stop them hooking on to obstructions.

Anchors

An anchor is a bit like a fire extinguisher, you never seem to notice it until you need it; and when you do, it is a matter of some urgency that it is going to do its job properly. It is likely to be a very bad day, you'll be out on a river, the engine has expired and the current is dragging the boat towards a weir; it'll probably start raining, just to rub it in, and the anchor is the only means of preventing what is merely an embarrassing situation from becoming a newspaper story.

To deploy the anchor, simply chuck it over the side furthest from the danger, play out the warp so it doesn't get tangled, then hang on tight and start praying. If the anchor bites hard into the river bed, the boat will swing around and stop, quite suddenly; and if your hand is between the anchor warp and the boat, you won't need to worry about cutting your finger nails again. The anchor may not bite at first, and will drag along the bed until it does; eventually (and this can be several miles if you are unlucky) it will catch and stop the boat, at which time you will be able to make repairs to the engine, scream for help, or quietly whimper under the bedclothes.

Removing the anchor from the river bed is a rather more difficult task. Once the boat is running again, you should be able to raise it by pulling it hard from exactly the opposite direction to the one in which it stuck. Often this is most easily done by driving the boat back along the path it took before you threw the anchor. Sometimes, however, the anchor

A good anchor is important.

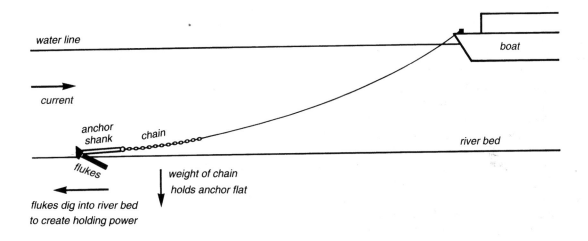

Anchor holding.

will have dug itself in so tightly that the only option is to cut it off and abandon it.

An anchor has a complex operation. The blades are designed to dig into the river bed at an angle sufficient to gain a firm purchase; this angle is set by the anchor's design, and also the weight of the chain. The chain's weight holds the top of the anchor against the ground, allowing the blades to drop down into the gravel or mud; the length of the chain and warp also allows this horizontal position to be achieved. If the warp is too short it will prevent the anchor blades achieving their optimum level for purchase.

For most narrow boats a 20lb (10kg) or 30lb (15kg) anchor is more than adequate; it should be secured to a welded link chain of 1–2in (2.5–5cm) link size, preferably galvanized, of the same weight. The anchor manufacturer will be able to advise on the most suitable anchor and chain weights for your particular boat. The other end of the chain is attached to a rope warp of sufficient diameter to take the required strain; this rope must be inspected regularly to ensure it is always ready for use. The length of the chain and warp is usually six fathoms (36ft/12m),

though it may well need to be varied on some rivers; a phone call to the relevant authority for details is a wise policy before cruising an unfamiliar river. The warp will need to be secured to the boat with a strong ring, and not just tied to a tee-stud.

On the canal system, anchors are seen as irrelevant to a boat's needs. This would be true enough if you never expected the boat to go on a river, but then who can foresee the future cruising range of a boat?

There is one further application for the anchor, namely when you need to moor the boat on a river in an area that is prone to vandalism. Such ruffians are not averse to untying the mooring ropes in the dead of night, and if they do this very quietly, the first you'll know about it is when you peer out of the window in the morning and discover the scenery is rather different. If you deploy the anchor on the off-side of the boat it will prevent you drifting too far away.

Navigation Lights

It is a requirement of the latest safety standards that newly built boats are fitted with a full set of navigation lights, port and starboard, a wide beam headlamp and a stern light. These are essential for night-time cruising and for navigating tunnels, and will need to be checked before a cruise. The headlamp is frequently knocked out of alignment in the course of normal cruising, so that as soon as you enter a tunnel you'll notice the beam pointing at the wall, the roof or the water – anywhere but where you want it. Thus before you enter a tunnel it is helpful to check that it is pointing in the right direction.

The authorities are not very enthusiastic about navigation at night, because in the dark it is so easy to forget to close paddles, and drain the cut. Nevertheless, cruising along a moonlit canal is one of the great pleasures of the waterways, and if you intend to do it regularly there are several additions to the boat that will make the experience easier and more fulfilling. A red light rather than a white one in the cockpit area will allow you to see the controls and gauges without reducing your night-time vision, rather like submarine conning towers. A remotely controlled, narrow beam searchlight mounted on the bows is a marvellous toy; you can pick out objects of interest such as species of wildlife, and keep them in the beam as you cruise by. Extra headlamps illuminating the area each side of the bows will improve the field of vision considerably, and make lock-working easier – although all this may make the boat look like a floating disco! A quiet engine and sensible regard for other boaters who may well be trying to get to sleep in their boats is only good manners.

Horn

The horn on a narrow boat needs to be a good loud one; the old-fashioned klaxons make a deafening noise when they are adjusted correctly, and no one is going to miss your sound signals if you use these! Motor car horns are also pretty loud, especially the air horns so favoured by boy racers. Horn signals are important if you have to navigate in dense fog or on a crowded waterway, as they enable you to inform other boats of your intentions, assuming they know what the signals mean. Just in case you've forgotten:

One short blast: 'I am turning to starboard';
Two short blasts: 'I am turning to port';
Three short blasts: 'I am reversing';
Four short blasts: 'I am unable to manoeuvre';
Four short and then one short: 'I am turning right round to starboard';
Four short and then two short: 'I am turning right round to port';
One long blast of ten seconds means 'I am here'; and is very useful when approaching blind corners and in dense fog; it can also concentrate the attention of another helmsman who is intent on watching the wildlife rather than the canal.

It is important to know these signals to avoid colliding with other boats.

First-Aid Kit

Every boat should carry a first-aid kit. It doesn't have to be a complicated affair, just a good supply of sterile bandages, wound dressing lotions and a box of elastoplast; there are plenty of sharp corners on boats and locks just waiting to inflict minor cuts and grazes on the unwary. An injury of more severity will need treatment by a qualified medical person. Some first-aid kits are so well equipped that the novice is tempted to remove an appendix just to get value for money from the kit. However, this isn't usually the correct treatment!

If you are taking small children on holiday an invaluable addition to the first-aid kit is a supply of oral rehydration salts; children can become so ill with an infection so quickly that within hours of becoming unwell they can't eat properly. These salt/sugar drinks will help to keep up their strength until you can get them to a doctor.

First-aid training is worthwhile.

Residential and Permanently Cruising Craft

Houseboats and boats which are constantly cruising have special needs when it comes to maintenance, since both fabric and fittings are placed under much more demanding conditions due to the boats' full-time occupation. Appliances will break down more frequently, the engine will need attention more often, and the humidity generated by people always on board will attack the woodwork more rapidly, particularly if ventilation is poor.

Boats on the move

Boats that are constantly cruising really need to be fitted with an engine that can be easily serviced. An interval of a hundred hours between services on an ordinary boat will probably mean a service once a year, whereas a boat that meanders a little way through the countryside each day may need a service once a month or less. This type of cruising puts the batteries through a far greater number of charge/discharge cycles, which reduces their overall life expectancy. On the whole such boats don't need a fixed generator on board since the main propulsion engine will be charging the batteries every day, and the cabin equipment using that power every evening.

If the boat does need 240-volt ac power for washing machines and similar equipment, it

Residential boats have special needs.

is possible to fit a small 240-volt alternator to the main engine, and use that to provide up to 5 kilowatts of power. This should be ample for most domestic appliances. However, these units place a considerable strain on the fan belt, and a handful of spares is invaluable.

Alternative Power Sources

Where prolonged stays are caused by stoppages or other crises, it doesn't take long to use up the batteries' power, and running the engine on tick-over for a couple of hours each day just to keep the batteries topped up is not very energy-efficient, or good for the motor. A lot of boats use wind generators and solar panels to good effect.

Wind generators will produce up to about 100 watts of power in good conditions – although good conditions for a wind generator are not generally considered as such by human beings; so when you get blown off the towpath by a gale at least you'll be able to console yourself with the thought of the batteries it will charge. Where a boat is moored can alter the performance of a unit dramatically; it will work best in winter weather, too – balmy summer breezes are pretty hopeless. An eight or ten foot (2.4–3m) mast is usually enough to raise the generator above any ground level obstructions; masts are available from the suppliers and can be stepped down for normal cruising. The bearings of the mast and rotor will require occasional lubrication, and the brushes on the top of the mast will need a clean every couple of years.

Photovoltaic panels are, conversely, a waste of space in the winter but fine in summer. They are mounted on the roof and directly convert sunlight to electricity, and the power output is limited only by how many panels you can afford. They aren't that cheap, but require no maintenance at all and should last at least a decade.

Waste-Holding Tanks

The nature of constant cruising usually means that ready cash is in short supply, and the expense of having a boat's waste-holding tank pumped out regularly can become onerous. To be economical, the boat needs as large a tank as possible; also, a pump can be fitted onto a separate outlet pipe so that the boat can empty the tank under its own power, and thus in time save a considerable sum. The pumps can be either a manual diaphragm type with a large bore, or an electric macerator; emptying a couple of hundred gallons of slurry by hand is hard work, and the electric one is a *much* easier way to do it. The installation is straightforward: the outlet pipe from the tank is cut and a 'Y' valve installed; this will allow either the normal pump-out pipe to connect to the tank, or the pump pipe. The pump outlet terminates in a second deck fitting with an internal thread. A 'lay flat' flexible pipe is fitted with the appropriate screw end, and runs from the pump to a foul water drain. Inside you simply turn on the pump and wait for the tank to empty, or crank the pump handle for an hour or two. The tank will want to be flushed through with plenty of fresh water to get all the waste out of both the tank and pipe, and the pipe will want a good rinse out before being coiled up and brought back on board.

Permanently Moored Boats

These floating cottages suffer from all the usual headaches of boats, with the possible exception of power supply and waste disposal systems. The steelwork of the hull is often completely ignored for years on end – no fresh paint, not even a scrub to remove the weeds – until left for long enough, the rust will eat its way through, and that will be that.

It is therefore important to keep on top of the hull maintenance, fitting sacrificial anodes, and painting. Ventilation of the interior is another vital component of their upkeep; each person on board will be breathing out a couple of pints of warm water a day, and there's nothing quite as good at encouraging wood rot.

Unusual Boating Tasks

Raising sunken boats can be fun, as long as it's someone else's boat. Boats do sink, although it is a rare occurrence. The classic way to sink a boat is to forget to replace the weed hatch after cleaning the propeller; the wash from the prop forces tons of water up into the boat, and glug, down she goes.

A far sadder way for a boat to sink is when it is just left to rot by an uncaring owner. The rain gets in, and as the years pass it settles down, the waste water outlets go under and the whole boat sinks; a sorry sight, especially once the local kids have slung bricks through all the windows. However, it does provide the opportunity for someone to pick up a very cheap boat for renovation!

On river navigations flooding leads to boats ending up with their sterns caught up on the bank; the waters subside, they can't float on an even keel, and they capsize.

It is also possible to sink a boat in a lock: the bows can be caught on a ledge on the top gates as the lock fills, or flooded by the rush of water from a gate paddle, or the stern can be caught on the sill as the water empties; though in most of these cases dropping the paddles quickly will prevent the boat going under.

The boat will probably be an obstruction to other craft, so it is important that the local Waterways staff know what has happened and what you intend to do. There will be a pollution hazard from the diesel oil in the

A boat sunk like this needs a professional salvage team.

tanks, and the insurance company will want to know all about it; also a photographic record will be useful in the event of an insurance claim. Refloating boats can be dangerous, so don't take any risks with your own safety. Never swim into an enclosed space on the boat, and never place yourself in a position where you could be trapped or crushed if the boat moves unexpectedly: hire a professional diver.

Luckily both narrow boats and canals have flat bottoms, and usually the canal's bottom isn't that far from the boat's! If a boat goes down it will probably only sink a foot or so, and will leave all the gunwales above the water-line; in this sort of position it is easy to refloat. The technique is to get into it and block off the route by which the water

entered; a second boat to work from, and to carry the pumping equipment, is usually essential.

This sort of work attracts plenty of gongoozlers who will need to be kept at a safe distance. A few friends to help make tea will render the task less daunting.

After the ingress of water has been prevented, get a pump working; a 2in (5cm) petrol-driven diaphragm pump should be able to lift the boat in an hour or two. As long as the pump removes the water faster than it gets in, the boat will eventually float. This is a simple process, unlike the entire refit that the boat will probably need if it's been sunk for more than a couple of days – the water will penetrate the woodwork and engine quickly, and if it isn't dried out fast, it will ruin everything. The engine will certainly need a complete overhaul if it has been submerged.

When a boat sinks in deeper water, in a deep canal or river, the problems multiply rapidly. Once the gunwales have submerged more than six inches the boat will need a professional salvage company with powerful lifting equipment. The gunwales can be built up with sand-bags for about six inches to allow the water to be extracted, and on most canals the water level can be dropped a certain amount by the Waterways staff. You won't be popular with them, but if it's the only way to re-open the navigation they really don't have much choice. If the boat is not sitting level on the canal or river bed, there is a strong chance that if anyone went on board to work on it, it could capsize; in this case call in professional help.

Summary

On the waterways, looking after a narrow boat is just as much a part of the way of life as working the locks and cruising along. Boats might come in all sorts of shapes and sizes, but each one has to be cared for individually in order to work to its optimum ability. Initially this might be hard work, but after a few years the needs of the boat will become second nature, and you'll find that it seems to look after itself. It doesn't of course, but *you* have reached the stage where repairs and maintenance are tackled so promptly that they never seem to become a problem. This idyllic state – Zen and the art of narrow boat maintenance – frees the boater to get on with the all-important task of cruising those beautiful waterways.

It's now time to start up the engine, cast off and potter away down the cut.

Useful Addresses

The Inland Waterways Association
PO Box 114
Rickmansworth WD3 1ZY
01923 711114

National Association of Boat Owners
Freepost BM8367
Birmingham B31 2BR

British Waterways Board
64 Clarendon Road
Watford
Hertfordshire WD17 1DA
01923 201120

British Marine Industry Federation
Marine House
Thorpe Lea Road
Egham
Surrey TW20 8BF

Canal Boatbuilders Association
(Address as for British Marine Industry
Federation)
0844 800 9575

Association of Waterway Cruising Clubs
The Yacht Basin
Camley Street
London NW1 0PL

Index